Allen W Chatfield

Songs and Hymns of Earliest Greek Christian Poets, Bishops and Others

translated into English verse

Allen W Chatfield

Songs and Hymns of Earliest Greek Christian Poets, Bishops and Others
translated into English verse

ISBN/EAN: 9783337735296

Printed in Europe, USA, Canada, Australia, Japan

Cover: Foto ©Thomas Meinert / pixelio.de

More available books at **www.hansebooks.com**

SONGS AND HYMNS

OF

Earliest Greek Christian Poets

BISHOPS AND OTHERS

Translated into English Verse

BY

ALLEN W. CHATFIELD, M.A.
VICAR OF MUCH MARCLE

RIVINGTONS
WATERLOO PLACE, LONDON
Oxford and Cambridge
1876

CONTENTS

	PAGE
PREFACE	v
SYNESIUS, CITIZEN OF CYRENE, AND BISHOP OF PTOLEMAÏS	1
I. ODE	7
II. ODE	14
III. ODE	19
IV. ODE	56
V. ODE	70
VI. ODE	75
VII. ODE	78
VIII. ODE	81
IX. ODE	84
X. ODE	88
GREGORY, BISHOP OF NAZIANZUS	91
I. HYMN TO CHRIST	93
II. HYMN TO GOD	98
III. HYMN TO CHRIST ON EASTER DAY (AFTER LONG SILENCE)	102
IV. SONG OR POEM TO HIS OWN SOUL	106
V. A MORNING PRAYER OR VOW	120
VI. FAILURE AS TO THE SAME	121
VII. AN EVENING HYMN	122
VIII. AN ADMONITORY POEM TO A VIRGIN	125

	PAGE
THE NAASSENI, A PSALM OF	137
METHODIUS, BISHOP AND MARTYR	139
VIRGINS' SONG	141
CLEMENT OF ALEXANDRIA	154
HYMN TO CHRIST	155
A POSTSCRIPT	159

VERY ANCIENT HYMNS OF UNKNOWN AUTHORSHIPS, LITERALLY RENDERED IN PROSE.

I. A MORNING HYMN	161
II. AN EVENING HYMN	164
III. A HYMN AT LAMP-LIGHT	165
IV. A PRAYER AT DINNER-TIME (OR GRACE BEFORE A MEAL)	166

ERRATA

Page 61, line 2, *for* "Father" *read* "Father's."
Page 138, line 2, *for* second "hither" *read* "thither."
Page 166, line 3, *for* "your" *read* "our."

PREFACE

FOUR years ago the *Anthologia Græca Carminum Christianorum* (Leipsic, 1871) was put into my hands by a friend, to look for hymns, Eucharistic especially, which, when rendered into English, might be suitable for the general use of the Church. Of Eucharistic hymns I did not find one in the volume. But I lighted frequently on detached passages here and there, which might form the groundwork of useful and popular hymns for general Christian worship. I did not then know that the late Dr. J. M. Neale had applied his magic wand to several of such passages which are to be found in the later portion of the *Anthologia*.

My attention, however, was at once arrested by the beauty and majesty of the earlier portion of the volume, which contains the Odes of Synesius, the Hymns and Songs of Gregory Nazianzen, a Hymn of Clement of Alexandria, and the Bridal Song of the earlier Methodius. In my humble opinion there is nothing in the second, the later, and by far the larger portion at all comparable in point of spirit or originality with what I have specified in the first short portion of the book. Moreover, all, or almost all, the later Greek Church poetry, or harmonious prose, which gradually took the place of the old poetry, is full of Mariolatry, of which I find nothing in the older portion referred to.

Such is the marvellous versatility of the Greek language and its power of *wort-bilden*, or compounding of words, that in or before the sixth century such words as θεοτόκος, θεομήτωρ, θεογεννήτωρ, came into general use; grammatically and beautifully formed, and logically too, so far as school logic is concerned; for if the Blessed Virgin is the mother of Him who is also God, she is, says such logic, the mother of God. Thus, by the genius of the language, aided by miserable school logic, the Blessed Virgin, the mother of the Man Christ Jesus, is made the mother of God; and as darkness and ignorance rapidly prevailed, so the worship of the Blessed Trinity is literally capped by the worship of the θεοτόκος, the prayer or doxology to the Virgin in each case forming the grand climax.[1]

Rome, as always in the old times, borrowed from Greece, and then stamped these and other monstrous departures from primitive truth with the seal of her own falsely assumed authority, and it became law like that of the Medes and Persians, which altereth not.

But let the descendants of the once noblest people on earth, the inheritors also of the glorious and divine treasures preserved in the old language—the finest ever spoken—let the Greek people and the Greek Church think and act with the mind unfettered; let them go back to the pure fountain and drink for themselves. The eye of the mind will be enlightened; they will see that neither Mariolatry, nor saint worship, nor angel worship, has any place in God's own truth. "See thou do it not," said the angel to St. John,[2] when he was about to fall down and

---

[1] See, for example, throughout the "Great Canon," by St. Andrew of Crete, the last stanza of each of the nine Odes, pp. 147-157.
[2] Rev. xxii. 9.

worship (only προσκυνῆσαι) before his feet. Oh that in obedience to such divine injunction the great Eastern Church would arise and shake itself from the dust; would cast to the moles and to the bats such relics of past darkness and idolatrous practice !

I was attracted also to the first part of the volume by the grand old Greek metres. To me they are vastly to be preferred to the later metrical or harmonious prose, or the mediæval and modern jingle. This last form of poetry may be required by the English and other modern languages which have not the metrical perfection natural to the old Greek and Latin tongues; but to adopt the modern fashion in reference to the ancient Greek and Latin seems to me an unnecessary and miserable distortion. That the old metres can express sublime thought and divine truth is abundantly attested by the Anacreontics of Synesius and Gregory. The dactylics also of the latter, his hexameters and pentameters, as well as his iambics, bear the same evidence.

How the change gradually took place in Greek poetry, how accent strangled quantity, and how harmonious prose succeeded to the grand old poetry, is elaborately set forth in the preface of the learned editors of the Greek *Anthology*. The same contains also a masterly essay on the music of the Greek Church.

I follow their order as convenient, though chronologically the reverse of what it ought to be, and place Synesius first.

MUCH MARCLE VICARAGE,
September 1, 1876.

SYNESIUS

BISHOP OF PTOLEMAÏS

(Born circ. A.D. 375, Died 430).

SYNESIUS was a man of mark in *his* day, and would have been a man of mark in *any* day.

To begin with the advantages which belonged to him by birth, he could boast a pedigree such as, says Gibbon, "could not be equalled in the history of mankind," of seventeen centuries from earliest heroic times, down through the kings of Sparta, and the founders of Cyrene: "all the names recorded in the public registers of Cyrene;" and he was well worthy of his " pure and illustrious pedigree."[1]

As a philosopher, his merits, measured by the standard of the age in which he lived, are of high

[1] See *The Decline and Fall of the Roman Empire*. Oxford edition, 1827, vol. ii. p. 446, and the foot notes. Also vol. iv. pp. 38, 39.

order. Otherwise, it is easy, in our age, to condemn the whole Neoplatonic philosophy as "tumid, inflated, and false."

As a statesman and patriot, he deserves the highest praise. For three years (A.D. 397–400) he toiled, as he himself tells us in his third Ode, and strove and wept at the court of Arcadius, endeavouring to stimulate his degraded and degenerate countrymen to worthy efforts against the Goths, who were threatening not only his own beloved Libya, but the whole empire. His noble appeal, and his continued exertions, called forth abundant commendation and praise, but no permanent results. "The court of Arcadius indulged the zeal, applauded the eloquence, *and* neglected the advice of Synesius."

But there must have been some lull in the rising storm, or some partial success; for Synesius expresses, in the ode referred to, his heartfelt thankfulness for the same. Certainly within the three following years considerable victories were gained by Stilicho in Italy. Hence may have arisen relief to Libya. And Synesius may have composed the Ode, or added the part referred to, after those events.

With regard to his Christianity and theological

views, it seems to me Synesius has had scant justice done to him. The learned editors of the *Anthologia* (see Prolegomena, p. x, lib. i., where *sex* must be a misprint for *quinque*) think that he had not yet even professed Christianity when he wrote *five* (viz. I. II. III. IV. VI.) out of the *ten* hymns or odes; that in the third, the very long one, he speaks of going round to *pagan* temples in supplication to the gods. But I would ask, had not pagan temples been put down *finally*, at least some years before Synesius visited Thrace? Whatever new life paganism may have received during the short reign of Julian (A.D. 360-363), it was crushed out during the reign of Theodosius the Great (A.D. 382-395). His sons divided the empire, Honorius reigning in the West, Arcadius in the East. It was to the court of Arcadius that Synesius went as a deputy from Cyrene. Again, may not Synesius be understood as speaking of Christian churches or temples, Christian ministers or guardian saints (in the growing notion of the day), and Christain rites and ceremonies, though employing in his poetry terms that in pagan times might have been applied to pagan worship? I am persuaded that it is so; and that, if not always orthodox, he yet shows himself in all these poems to be a reverent and sincere Christian.

I cannot enter at length into the famous dispute as to what Synesius held, or did not hold, on the doctrine of the Resurrection. It has been commonly said that he did not accept it at all. Gibbon reiterates the same; and in reply to Bishop Jeremy Taylor and others, who, I believe rightly, qualify this, thinking that Synesius dissembled, or represented his difficulties too strongly, in order that he might not be forced into the holy office, Bingham[1] quotes and interprets, but I think not fully nor fairly, the words of Synesius himself: τὴν καθωμιλημένην ἀνάστασιν ἱερόν τι καὶ ἀπόρρητον ἥγημαι, καὶ πολλοῦ δέω ταῖς τοῦ πλήθους ὑπολήψεσιν ὁμολογῆσαι . . . . Surely there is much qualification here. "The every-day-talked-of resurrection I have regarded as a sacred thing, and that cannot be spoken of." He does not say that he does not believe it at all, but that, whereas it is in every one's mouth, stated and defined, he has been in the habit of regarding it as a sacred and ineffable mystery; and that he is far from acceding to the notions of the multitude (on it or other points).

[1] *Christian Antiquities*, vol. i. pp. 464-5, London edition, 1843.

That he held the doctrine itself is to me clear, from what he himself says, both elsewhere, and particularly in his beautiful tenth Ode. He believes in, and adores, the *risen* Saviour, and looks forward with longing desire in the future state to be with Him, and to "sing His praise who is the Healer of souls and the Healer of limbs, with the Great Father and the Holy Spirit." I know not how Mosheim can call such a man a semi-Christian.[1] Mosheim's translator and annotator[2] does something in the way of correcting or qualifying such judgment.

It is certain that, when later in life (viz. A.D. 410) he was made Bishop of Ptolemaïs, Synesius acquitted himself nobly and faithfully in the sacred office to which, entirely against his will, he had been appointed. "The philosophic bishop supported with dignity the character which he had assumed with reluctance."[3]

All admit that he was a man of learning and wisdom, of excellent character, and blameless life. His refinement of mind, his delicacy of feeling, and his loving disposition, as well as his zeal and energy, must strike

[1] See *Ecclesiastical History*. London edition, 1845, vol. i. pp. 310, 439.
[2] See the Notes, ibid.
[3] GIBBON, *Decline and Fall*, vol. ii. p. 446.

every attentive reader. I would specially refer to his eighth Ode, in which is presented to us a picture of conjugal, parental, and domestic tenderness, that nowhere can be surpassed.

His poetry in the original Greek will be allowed by all scholars to be pure, varied, sweet, and beautiful.

Much must be lost in any translation whatever. If I may have had only slight success in attempting to reproduce to the English reader the mind of this good and great man, I shall indeed be thankful.

Synesius.

I.

"Ἄγε μοι, λίγεια φόρμιγξ,

(*Anacreontic: Dimeter ionic.*)

WAKE, wake, I pray thee, shrill-toned lyre!
No more to fan the Teïan[1] fire,
No more the Lesbian[2] strain to raise,
Wake, wake to hymn of nobler praise!
Sound Dorian[3] ode, in other guise,
Than once to maid with laughing eyes,
Or youth whose form and golden tresses
Might woo the wanton air's caresses!
A better theme inspires my song,
And bears my soul far hence along. 10
A Virgin's God-conceiving throes,
Wisdom's own cure for mortal woes—

---

[1] Anacreon was of Teos.
[2] Sappho of Lesbos.
[3] The Dorian dialect was generally used for graver and sublimer subjects.

This bids me now my harp-strings ply,
And earth's black loves and miseries fly.
For what is strength, or beauty's sway,
Or gold, or fame—what doth it weigh—
Or royal honours—in the scale?
What these 'gainst search for God avail?
Let this man urge the well-horsed car,
That shoot the true-aimed arrow far;   20
Another watch o'er golden heap,
And safe his hoarded treasure keep;
To one be pride of glossy hair
Flowing o'er neck in wavelets fair;
Another court the favouring glances
Of boys and girls in hymns and dances.
Not such for me! But this I pray,
Unknown to spend life's quiet day;
To this vain world unmarked, unknown,
But God's truth knowing as my own.   30
Wisdom present herself to me!
Good guide of youth and age is she,
Of wealth good stewardess and queen,
Alike in poverty serene;
Beyond earth's sorrows smiling gay,
To calm content she points the way.

That priceless wisdom first I ask,
To guide and sweeten all life's task,
And then sufficient humble store
To keep me from my neighbour's door ; 40
That I may ne'er, oppressed with need,
Harbour dark thoughts of selfish greed.

Hark ! 'tis the sweet cicada's song :
He drinks the dew, and chirps along.
And, lo ! my strings unbidden sound,
And here and there a voice around !
What in the world—what melody
Will pang divine bring forth to me ?

'Tis so ! Self-sprung Beginning He,
Father and Lord of all that be : 50
Not made, not born, on high alone
He hath o'er lofty heaven His throne.
There glory changeless He displays,
And sceptre there eternal sways ;
Of unities pure Unity,
And Sole of sole existence He !
High ether pure He did combine,
And quicken into Life Divine.

He then, ere yet the ages ran,
In mode ineffable to man,   60
The Godhead through the Firstborn poured :[1]
Hence Three, yet One, the Triune Lord.

And now the heavenly fount around
Behold, with children's beauty crowned,
Forth from the centre as they spring,
Or round it flow in joyous ring.

But stop, rash lyre, thy lofty flight,
Nor touch things hid from mortal sight!
To men below it is not given
To tell high mystic rites of heaven.   70
The things beneath do thou reveal;
The things above let silence seal.

But Mind now cares for worlds alone,
In which reflected mind is shown:
A good beginning this we sing,
For thence man's spirit hath its spring:

---

[1] Lit.: The Sole Unity poured forth through the first-sown Form in an ineffable way had a threefold supreme help.

For now to matter came there down
Mind incorruptible, high crown,
Severed in each, and fragment small,
Yet true descent from God of all. 80
This whole, in every part one-centred,
Whole into whole as it hath entered,
Takes station at the eternal poles,
And heaven's resplendent circle rolls.
Divided next, to those again,
In given form who yet retain
Their dowry unimpaired of mind,
There are high offices assigned ;
The chariot race of stars one guides,
One o'er the angelic choir presides. 90
But, ah ! another, empty, vain,
Self-dragged by down-inclining chain,
Hath found a form of lower earth,
Deep fallen from his heavenly birth :
From home apostate far he flew,
And cups of Lethe's darkness drew ;
Of eyeless soul and murky mind,
To heaven's true joy and glory blind ;
Fain he to joyless earth repaired,
A god by mortal things ensnared. 100

All dark ! yet, lo ! to mortal eyes
A ray of cheering light doth rise !
A door of hope is opened high,
And helping hand is stretched out nigh,
To lift the fallen here on earth
Back to the honours of their birth,
When they, emerging from the strife
And din and cares of storm-tossed life,
To holy paths have turned indeed,
Which to their Father's palace lead.   110
Blest he who from the entangling mesh
Of matter and of greedy flesh
Hath fled, and on with springing bound
The upward way to God hath found !
Blest he who, after fates severe,
And toils and many a bitter tear,
And all the crowd of anxious cares
Which earth to all her votaries shares,
To mind's true course at length restored,
Hath God's own shining depth explored !   120

A task it is, to lift above
Whole outstretched soul in new-born love !

Yet only make determined start,
With wings of mind and honest heart,
And nigh to thee will He appear
With stretched-forth hands, thy Father dear.
Before will run a shining light,
And all thy upward paths make bright :
Fields of sweet thought thou now shalt tread,
Pledge of true beauty, for thee spread ! 130
Come, O my soul, and drink of this,
A fountain flowing with all bliss ;
And to thy Father, lifting prayer,
Without delay, up-mount the air.
Leaving to earth the things of earth,
In God assert thy godlike birth ;
And mingling with thy Father, Friend,
Taste joys above that never end.

Synesius.

II.

Πάλι φέγγος, πάλιν ἀώς,

(*Anacreontic: Dimeter ionic.*)

AGAIN we hail the opening morn,
Again breaks forth the day new-born,
Which, rising in victorious might,
Chases away black-wandering night !
Again, my mind, in early songs
Praise Him to whom all praise belongs ;
Who gave to morning dawn the light
Who gave the glittering stars to night,
Which to their Maker and their King
Around the world in chorus sing.   10
For o'er prolific matter, high,
Moves ether pure in fiery sky ;
Where glides the moon in glorious trim,
Cutting the last encircling rim :

For to the eighth revolving stream
The star-borne courses brightly gleam.
But now beyond the starry poles
A counter sea of glory rolls,
Unbosomed; and with dance divine
Doth the Eternal Mind enshrine,   20
Which covered hath with hoary wings
The palace of the King of kings.
What is beyond none may relate,
Nor mind of man can penetrate :
Eternal severance restrains,
And happy silence ever reigns.
From Root, or Spring, or Fountain one
A threefold lighted Form hath shone :
For where the Father dwells above,
There dwelleth too His own heart's love,   30
His glorious Son, wisdom perfect,
And of all worlds the Architect :
And in the Unity combined
The Spirit's holy Light hath shined.
One Root of Good, one Fount of Love,
Whence sprung the bliss supreme above :
And the bright holy lamps divine
In equal glory ever shine.

And thence in this fair world of ours,
With high-born intellectual powers, 40
A chorus now of deathless kings
The Triune glory ever sings.
And near the Fount of Love and Truth
Angelic band in changeless youth,
Guided by holy Wisdom's mind,
Immortal wreath of beauty find.
But some with dark averted eyes
Fall mindless from the lofty skies
Downward the gloomy depths among,
And bring the higher world along; 50
Down, down to Matter's utmost bound,
Where, settling in the depth profound,
Nature assigns them birth and place,
A God-like,[1] though God-fallen race.

Hence giant heroes took their birth,
The mighty conquerors of earth;
And hence Breath sown o'er all the ground
Each varying type of life hath found.
But all things to Thy counsel hold,
Things past, or present, new or old: 60

[1] Lit: A much-talking and much-plotting crowd of demons (i. e. demigods).

Whate'er we have, whate'er we share,
Of all from Thee the sources are.
The Father and the Mother Thou,
Male, female, unto Thee we bow:
Or voice be heard, or all be still,
'Tis just as ordered by Thy will.
And Thou or Nature Thyself art,
Or Nature is Thy counterpart:
And Thou art King; and ages all
Within Thine age unmeasured fall. 70
May I my song aright renew,
O Thou, the Root whence all things grew!
Hail! Thou, the world's Original;
Hail! Thou, the Spring, First Cause of all.
All numbers blending into one,
The Uncreated, God alone!
All hail, all hail,[1] Thou One Divine!
All joy, all happiness be Thine!
Bend Thou, O bend propitious ear,
And this my hymn of praises hear, 80
Speed on true Wisdom's opening day,
Pour blessings down in rich array:

---

[1] χαῖρε—χαίροις—χαίρειν. We cannot imitate in English the beautiful play on these words.

Yea, grace-distilling streams pour down,
That I may win contentment's crown
In life's sweet calm; the happy mean
Give me, riches and want between.
Off from my limbs diseases ward,
My soul from stormy passions guard :
Let no dark thoughts my steps attend :
My life from biting cares defend ;   90
Lest mind, borne down by earthly ill,
To soar should find nor time nor will.
But grant me with free wing to rise,
And join the chorus of the skies,
And there with Thine for ever sing
The glories of my God and King !

Synesius.

III.[1]

Ἄγε μοι ψυχὰ

(*Anapæstic monometer.*)

1. (1-11).

LIFT up thyself, my soul,
Above this world's control !
Spend and be spent in holy hymns of praise :
Be armed with pure desire,
Burn with celestial fire :
Unto the King of gods our voice we raise :
To Him a crown we weave, and bring
A sacrifice of words, a bloodless offering.

[1] In the Greek, however short the metre and however long the ode, there is no weariness from monotony; for the interchange of anapæst, dactyl, and spondee, in the lines of from only four to six syllables each, makes a constant and pleasing variety. But this being impossible in an English translation, I have adopted the measure which Milton so beautifully employs in the Hymn of the Nativity. For the convenience of those who may wish to refer to the original, I mark the lines at the head of each stanza.

II. (11–22).

Thee on the troubled deep,
Thee o'er the islands steep,
Thee through the mighty continents of land,
    Thee in the city's throng,
    Or mountain tops along,
Or when in celebrated plains I stand,
    Thee, Thee, O blessed One, I sing,
Thee, Thee, O Father of the world, Eternal King!

III. (23–36).

Thy praise I hymn by night,
Thy praise at morning light,
Thy praise by day, Thy praise at eventide.
    This know the hoary stars,
    And moon with silver bars,
And chiefly he that doth on high preside
    O'er all the host of heaven, the sun,
Who measuring time for holy souls his course doth run.

IV. (37–50).

    Fain to thy folds I sped,
    And to Thy bosom fled,
Winging my steps from Matter's wide-spread rule:
    Now on famed mountain peak,
    Thy face alone to seek;
Now on the plain I hailed thy vestibule.
    A suppliant thus to many a shrine
Of sacred rites I came, and mysteries divine.

V. (51–67).

    And now to southern land,
    And Libya's desert strand
I roamed, where neither godless spirit reigns,
    Nor teeming cities' strife
    Calls men to busy life;
That so my soul, from woeful toils and pains
    And passions' war and groans set free,
And all the ills of fate, might harmonize with Thee.

VI. (68–75).

And might, in blest relief,
Unshackled now from grief,
With lips and tongue all cleansed, and hallowed mind,
Repay the hymn to Thee,
The hymn full due from me.
Be Earth and Ether holily combined
And Air and Sea with one accord
Be still, and join in adoration to the Lord!

VII. (76–85).

Swift breath of winds, be still,
And whirling pool and rill,
And floods that are at rivers' mouths forth hurled;
And streams from fountain-heads
That rush down rocky beds:
And hushed be ye, deep hollows of the world;
While breath in holy hymns is spent,
And sacrifice of praise in upward strains is sent.

VIII. (86–94).

Down sink the serpent's trail!
  Nor let their craft prevail!
Down sink the wingèd dragon underground;
  Who loves to cloud the soul,
  The god who doth control
This lower world, and idol-worship found,
  And urgeth on the dogs of hell
Against God's praying people, His true Israel!

IX. (95–107).

  O blessèd Father, Friend,
  My soul do Thou defend
From soul-devouring dogs; defend my prayer,
  Defend my deeds, my life,
  From their destructive strife:
And charge Thy holy angels, that they bear
  To Thee this offering of my mind:
For hymns they carry that with Thee acceptance find.

X. (108–117).

Now am I borne along
To lists of sacred song:
Now holy words in streams spontaneous flow:
 A voice within me rings,
 And toucheth my heart-strings:
But unto me, O Father, mercy show;
 Forgive, O Blessèd, if I stray,
In theme divine, and miss the rightful ordered way.

XI. (118–125).

What eye can steadfast gaze,
When Thy dread beacons blaze?
What eye so wise, so strong, of mortal man,
 That it unclosed may bear
 Thy vivid lightning's glare?
E'en of the mighty ones on high none can,
 However strong, however bold,
The glorious brightness of Thy Majesty behold.

XII. (126–137).

Now aims the mind too far,
And finds repelling bar,
Nor can it penetrate by utmost strain
    The depths so dazzling bright,
    Where Thou dost dwell in light:
So, falling back from efforts feebly vain,
    It courts within its proper scope
An object known whereon to fix the eye of hope;

XIII. (138–146).

That for Thy hymns it might
Thence pluck fair flowers of light,
Nor leave to thankless winds an offering:
    But render back to Thee
    Thine own, for Thine they be;
For what of all things is not Thine, O King?
    O Father of all fathers, Thou!
To Thine eternal Fatherhood all beings bow!

XIV. (147-157).

But Father Thou hadst none;
Thou art the self-sprung One,
Before all worlds the sole great Mind existing:
Germ of whate'er we see,
Spur of all things that be:
Root of first worlds, by Thee alone subsisting:
Light of all light, Truth's basis sure;
And Wisdom's everflowing stream, and fountain pure.

XV. (158-165).

O Mind immutable!
O Light inscrutable!
Thine is the eye that guides the lightning fire:
In Thee the ages live,
Thou dost their limits give;
Who can Thy praises reach, Eternal Sire?
Thou art beyond the dreams of men;
Beyond the reach of mind, or highest angel's ken.

XVI. (166-173).

    O'er all Thy rule is spread,
    The living and the dead;
To minds that be, the parent Mind Thou art;
    All heaven Thou dost control,
    Thou nourishest the soul,
And dost to spirit energy impart;
    The Spring Thou art whence all things flow,
And from eternity the Root whence all things grow.

XVII. (174-183).

    The only One, yet all;
    In Thee all numbers fall;
The only One, yet countless evermore:
    The self-existent Mind,
    Yet mind with law combined;
Mind's realm, yet all the realm of mind before:
    Through all, yet all beyond, art Thou:
To Thee, the Seed of all existing things, we bow.

XVIII. (184-190).

 Thou art the Eternal Root,
 Thou art the spreading Shoot!
Or male or female Thou be called, 'tis one;
 To mind Thou nature art,
 And dost Thyself impart,
But mind enlightened ne'er can say, 'tis done;
 But here and there a word outpours,
While feebly it the unfathomed depth around explores.

XIX. (191-198).

 Thou art the Parent Tree,
 All have their life from Thee,
Or stem or branch, whatever is, is Thine.
 Thou art the Light of light,
 The Light of day so bright,
The Light that shineth evermore Divine:
 Thou art, again, the hidden Light,
By its own glory hidden far from mortal sight.

XX. (199–209).

Yet one, yet all, one Lord,
One only, yet forth poured,
Through all forth poured in holy Mystery:
Of Thee thus sprung the Son,
Wisdom, the glorious One,
Creator of the universe to be.
The Godhead severed into twain
By birth ineffable, unsevered doth remain.

XXI. (210–216).

Yet One, though Twain, though Three:
Mysterious Trinity!
For Thou art One in Three, and Three in One.
I sing Thee, Unity!
I sing Thee, Trinity!
The Triune King, the Father, Spirit, Son!
The Light divided is not spent,
The One pervading mind, though parted, is not rent.

XXII. (217-224).

 Thy holy Will is done,
 'Tis through the Eternal Son;
And from the outpoured Godhead forth there springs,
 Which cannot be exprest
 In words, the Spirit Blest,
The Uncreated! we of wondrous things
 Have spoken; but we speak not *there:*
We dare not if we could, we could not if we dare.

XXIII. (225-231).

 Who knows the Eternal Laws?
 Who knows the First Great Cause?
We may not say a Second, or a Third.
 O Birth beyond our reach;
 O Spring defying speech!
What mortal to the task himself could gird?
 O matchless Holy One, between
The Father and the Son Thy Light doth intervene.

XXIV. (232–240).

All reverence to Thee,
Eternal Spirit, be!
Thou of the Three the middle rank dost hold.
And now, most glorious Son,
Thy praises be begun!
Thy birth, thy generation, is untold:
The Father's Son, the Father's Will,
With Him Thou present wast, and present Thou art still.

XXV. (241–253).

Thou with the Father art,
And ever next His heart;
Nor can deep flowing Time Thy birth reveal;
Nor aged Æon say
When was Thy natal day;
He never learned, nor could remove the seal.
Son with the Father! He the same
Who should hereafter give to Æon birth and name.

XXVI. (254-265).

 Who hath adjudged the eye
 Into God's depths to pry?
The subtle tongue will dare, but man is blind.
 Such daring is in vain,
 'Tis godless and profane.
Thou dost to Thine pour light upon the mind,
 And guard their hearts with holy care,
That they in darkness sink not through gross matter's
  snare.

XXVII. (266-275).

 To Thee all holy praise
 It well befits to raise;
For Thou of all art Father, all are Thine:
 Thou all the worlds didst found,
 Thou dost all ages bound,
Thou framedst all the host of heaven divine;
 To Thee all minds of light do sing,
And starry spheres intelligent hail Thee their King!

XXVIII. (276–285).

 While round in holy choir
 Dance their bright orbs of fire,
The blest ones all do shout and sing before Thee;
 The world within, around,
 They all Thy praise resound,
All in their stations evermore adore Thee:
 Those in the zones; and those outside,
Who yet their several posts assigned in wisdom guide.

XXIX. (286–300).

 These come to guard, or tame,
 Earth's helmsmen, sons of fame;
Of link angelic, and who draw their birth
 From old heroic race;
 Who ever take their place,
By hidden ways, o'er men and things of earth:
 And though of an unyielding will,
To dark-rayed worldly glories ever yield they still.

XXX. (301-311).

To Thee blithe nature sings,
And all from her that springs:
For Thou with heavenly breath dost them renew,
Forth pouring from above
Thy stores of grace and love,
Which ever fresh descend in showers and dew;
Thou to all nature nature art,
O Lord of worlds unstained! and dost Thine own impart.

XXXI. (312-319).

For nature Thou didst train
And school, that she again
Might parent be of every mortal thing;
The faithful counterpart
Of all that Thyself art,
Of life and health the everflowing spring!
That to the world's extremest bound
Each part in turn with living beauty might be crowned.

XXXII. (320–328).

  For it were never right
  That things should jar and fight,
Or dregs of earth with excellence contend;
  But all by Thy decree
  Is wrought in harmony;
Nor aught shall perish, nor the chorus end;
  But each from other takes its share,
And all through one another taste Thy loving care.

XXXIII. (329–334).

  The eternal wheel revolves,
  And the dark riddle solves;
Things die; Thou sendest forth Thy breath, they
  live,
  And in fresh glory bloom,
  Renewed from mortal doom.
Thus nurtured nature nurturing doth give;
  And she doth sing a deathless song
To Thee by all her children through the ages long.

XXXIV. (335-342).

In colour or in skin
Without, or life within,
And deeds, however varied they may be,
Yet nature moulds them all
Obedient to her call,
And links them fast in holy unity;
And from all creatures thus doth raise
Of differing voices one harmonious hymn of praise.

XXXV. (343-357).

To Thee, their Lord and King,
All things their tribute bring
Of ceaseless praise; the night, the morn, the sky,
The lightning flash, the snow,
And things that spring and grow;
All bodies and all spirits; birds that fly,
And beasts that graze; seeds, plants, and roots;
The sea with all that swims, and earth with all her
fruits.

XXXVI. (358-367).

The waves of trouble roll;
Look Thou upon my soul,
To act so powerless, to learn so slow,
Where on Thy Libyan sands
The mystic temple stands;
For hither I, Thy holy will to know,
Oppressed with grief, my steps have bent,
On prayer and supplication unto Thee intent.

XXXVII. (368-374).

Before Thy favouring eye
Earth's gloomy vapours fly:
Look Thou on me, and bid my sorrows cease.
'Tis so! e'en now my heart
Through food Thy hymns impart—
For Thine they are—hath nourishment of peace,
And points my mind with keen desire
To rise afresh to thoughts and words of heavenly fire.

XXXVIII. (375–380).

But send, O King, Thy light,
To quicken my dull sight,
And guide me on the road that leads to Thee.
And, Father, grant, I pray,
That from the body's sway
My better part, escaping, may be free,
  And not again be downward hurled
Beneath the floods and eddies of this troubled world.

XXXIX. (381–391).

Yet here, while in the strife
Of world-enchainèd life,
O Blessèd, may kind fortune smile on me;
Nor stormy tempest blow
To check the holy glow,
Or rudely break the mind's tranquillity;
  Lest inrush of the worldly flood
Should leave to me no leisure for the things of God.

XL. (392–401).

And whereto I have striven,
By grace which Thou hast given,
(For all good gifts of help and strength are Thine),
May I the ground retain,
Nor e'er fall back again.
For which Thy gifts this humble wreath of mine
From holy fields to Thee I bring,
O Thou of all creations pure the Eternal King;

XLI. (402–409).

To Thee and to Thy Son,
Thine own, the only One,
Alone of Thee begotten, the All-wise,
Whom from eternity
Thou hadst, and hast, with Thee,
Though forth from Thee He came to harmonize
All things, and fashion, form, and guide,
By wisdom's breath outpoured, and over all preside.

XLII. (410–416).

    The hoary ages wake,
    And their due courses take,
At his command; and of His matchless skill,
    And workmanship divine,
    As if by plumb and line,
This rugged world He mouldeth to His will,
  Whate'er exists above the ground,
Or on its surface, or within its depths profound.

XLIII. (417–427).

    And merciful and kind
    He shines with holy mind
On toiling mortals; and doth bring relief;
    For He doth loose the chain
    Of toilsome care and pain;
Effects their good; and drives away their grief.
  The God who did the world create,
What marvel that His own He guard from whelming fate?

XLIV. (428–440).

And hither southward now,
  That I might pay this vow
To Thee the mighty world's eternal guide,
  I came from northern Thrace,
  Where three years' dreary space
Near the Imperial Court I did abide,
  In toil, with tears and anguish sore,
For on my shoulders I my mother country bore.

XLV. (441–454).

And well Thou know'st, good Lord,
  How from my limbs was poured
A sweat of agony from day to day:
  Nor rest had I by night
  In that dire mental fight:
But watered was the couch on which I lay
  From streaming eyes. Then to and fro,
To every shrine a suppliant I made haste to go.

XLVI. (455–462).

To all in turn I bring
Prayer, chaplet, offering,
And water with my tears each sacred floor,
That I might not with pain
Have journey made in vain,
But that Thou wouldst wide-open hopeful door.
Thus in my own and country's need
I with Thy holy ones through fruitful Thrace did plead;

XLVII. (463–473).

And who across the main,
Guard Carthaginian plain,
I sought them all, if they might succour me,
Throughout the region round,
Whom Thou with rays hadst crowned
Angelic, Thine attendant saints to be.
The blest ones helped my eager prayers,
They helped my many toils, and soothed my many cares.

XLVIII. (474-489).

Life did no pleasure yield,
    While my poor country reeled
Half stunned: but Thou hast righted her, O King!
    The Rock of Ages Thou,
    To whom the world doth bow!
Crushed were my limbs, my soul a lifeless thing:
  But Thou from Heaven hast breathed at length
New vigour on my soul, and on my limbs new strength.

XLIX. (490-497).

For Thou hast brought relief,
    And stayed o'erflowing grief:
Toils have an end, the wearied soul hath rest.
    'Twas by Thy wisdom planned,
    'Twas wrought out by Thy hand.
Thou to my mind hast given refreshment blest.
  Now, O my God, do Thou ordain,
That to the Libyans these Thine own sweet gifts remain;

L. (498–505).

    Of our long tribulation,
    Of Thy so great Salvation,
A lasting record! Hear Thy suppliant's prayer;
    And henceforth may my life
    Be safe from harmful strife.
Loose me from toil, disease, and deadly care.
    Thus to Thy servant bow Thine ear,
And grant my mental life be ever bright and clear.

LI. (506–523).

    I would not showers of wealth
    To try the soul's best health,
And leave no leisure for the things divine;
    Nor poverty would I,
    With downcast sullen eye,
Black spectre to the house, prone to repine,
    Bowed down to earth with earthly cares.
Both grovel on the ground, and both are dangerous
    snares.

LII. (524-532).

And both forgetful are
Of better things by far,
The mind, and all that to the mind doth cling,
Unless, O heavenly Friend,
Thou shouldst Thy help extend.
Yea, Father, wisdom's holy self and spring,
Upon this faltering soul of mine
The light of mind from Thine own bosom cause to shine.

LIII. (533-543).

And on my heart, I pray,
Turn Thou blest wisdom's ray,
With helping hand, and point the holy road
That leadeth unto Thee;
And set Thy seal on me,
And let me have the token of my God;
And from my life, and from my prayer,
Drive earthly demons of presumption and despair.

LIV. (544-553).

And may my body be
From all dishonour free,
As fortress unassailable to foe;
And may my spirit pure
Unto the end endure
By Thine all-saving help. Full well I know,
  That I do bear dark worldly stain,
And held in bondage am by earthly passions' chain;

LV. (544-563).

But Thou deliverer art,
And cleanser of the heart.
From evils circling round escape afford,
  And from diseases all,
  And bonds that fret and gall.
I bear Thy seed, of noble mind, good Lord,
  A spark that issued forth from Thee,
And flashing down through depths of matter lit on me.

LVI. (564–574).

For in the world, O King,
Thou mad'st a soul to spring,
And in the body, through the soul, a mind :
O pity then Thine own,
The handmaid from Thy throne :
From Thee descending, hapless I did bind
   Myself as labourer free to earth :
Not labourer now, but slave, downfallen from my
   birth.

LVII. (575–585).

For, me the world around
With witchery hath bound,
Some little strength may yet remain in me
Of secret inner light,
Not yet extinguished quite :
But o'er my head is rolled a mighty sea,
   That doth make blind the mental eye
That would its God and things of heavenly worth
   descry.

LVIII. (586–592).

  O look with pitying eye,
  And hear the mournful cry
Of Thine own child, O Father good and kind:
  Whom oft when she would rise
  Up to her native skies,
Impelled by holy efforts of the mind,
  Yet fascination of this world
Hath choked, and back to earth's dark mazes hurled.

LIX. (593–602).

  But O! send forth Thy light,
  A beacon fire through night,
To guide and cheer me on my upward way;
  And may that seed take root,
  And, striking out its shoot
From small beginning, head of flower display.
  O Father, such Thy help divine,
Enthrone me in the light of life above to shine;

LX. (603-611).

Where nature cannot clasp
    With her resistless grasp :
And whence no longer earth, or web of fate,
    Can back recall to woe
    And vain desires below.
Let brood deceitful that I scorn and hate
  Of worldly passions scattered be,
And leave thy servant, O my God, at peace with Thee!

LXI. (612-627).

Me and earth's din betwixt
    Be fiery barrier fixed.
Thy grace, O Father, to my soul reveal ;
    And let thy suppliant find,
    With outspread wings of mind,
The ascending path, and bear aloft Thy seal,
  A terror to the up-springing foe,
Who breathe to mortals godless thoughts from depths below ;

LXII. (628-635).

But badge and token known
To those about Thy throne,
The holy ones, who all the heights survey
Of Thy bright world, and stand
As guards in high command,
Bearing the keys of upward fiery way,
That they may give an entrance free,
And open wide the gates of heavenly light to me.

LXIII. (636-645).

But still while creeping here
Upon this empty sphere
Of earth, yet not of earth grant me to be;
But from a better root
E'en here attesting fruit
To bear of fire-proved deeds, my God, to Thee;
And Thy true voice to hear and know,
And whate'er warms and makes in souls blest hope to grow.

LXIV. (646-653).

It doth me now repent
    Of life on earth ill-spent :
Begone, the blear-eyed haze of godless men,
    And built-up cities' strength :
    Begone, ye breadth and length
Of worldly aims, nor harass me again,
    Ye sweet calamities, ye toys
Of mighty seeming, bootless boons, and joyless joys.

LXV. (654-661).

Tranced by your bravery
    The soul in slavery
To earth is held; and wretched is indeed ;
    For of her own good things
    This cup oblivion brings :
And things, wherewith to satisfy her need
    She hoped, are forthwith snatched away ;
And from vain dream she wakes to envy's shaft a
    prey.

LXVI. (662–670).

For fortune here below
A double face doth show,
False queen: whom if you haply win and trust,
And in her livery shine,
And at her table dine,
Soon rue your lot with bitter tears you must,
   When down from pedestal so high
You fall in widespread ruin, and neglected lie.

LXVII. (671–683).

For here, from adverse sides,
Now good, now ill, betides:
To mortals such is life's necessity.
To God, or what hath birth
From God, but not to earth,
Is good unmingled with adversity.
   Did cup of sweets intoxicate?
Ensnared I learnt by crop of woes a lesson late.

LXVIII. (684–693).

I hate these laws of change ;
And hence now upward range,
With wings expanded, to the peaceful sky :
To bright ethereal plains,
Where my dear Father reigns,
From earth, and earth's two-sided gifts I fly.
O Steward of the life of mind,
To Thee I look ; with Thee may I acceptance find.

LXIX. (694–703).

My soul doth hang on Thee :
Heed Thou Thy suppliant's plea,
Bound here on earth, yet struggling to ascend
The upward paths of mind :
As Thou thus far hast shined,
O shine yet more : light wings of succour lend :
Snap double passions' bond, and chain
Of earth unloose, and let my soul her freedom gain.

LXX. (704–713).

    For nature by these chains
    Her treacherous power obtains,
And binds me down to earth a helpless prey;
    But from the body freed,
    And all its direful need,
Grant me to take swift flight to realms of day,
   To Thine own halls and Thine own breast,
Whence flows the Fountain of the soul; and be at rest.

LXXI. (714–725).

    A drop from Fountain Head
    Poured forth, to earth I sped,
An exile and a wanderer from Thee;
    Me now, I pray, restore
    To where I was before:
With light ancestral may I mingled be!
   Tune Thou my mind with Thine own choir
In holiness to sing the hymns Thou dost inspire.

LXXII. (726-734).

Once saved from mortal plight,
Once mingled with the light,
O Father, grant I never enter more
　Within earth's black domains
　Of penalties and pains;
But while I yet am chained to this dark shore,
　And bear life's drudgery below,
Bid Thou that fortune's breezes on me gently blow.

Synesius.

IV.

Σὲ μὲν ἀρχομένας,

(*Anapæstic monometer.*)

1. (1-9).

To THEE at evening gray,
To Thee at growth of day,
To Thee at noon, to Thee at vesper hour,
  And when now fades the light,
  And poured forth is the night,
(Both night and day are Thine, and show Thy power),
  I sing, O Healer of the soul,
And of the body too: Thou only mak'st it whole.

II. (10–17).

And wisdom's spring Thou art,
And dost of it impart;
And Thou dost drive diseases far away,
And unto souls dost give
Untroubled life to live,
Which earthly care may not stamp down nor sway,
Who mother is of pain and woe,
And all the thousand ills that culminate below.

III. (18–27).

From which O grant to me
My life be ever free!
That I may praise in thankful hymn and song
The hidden Root of all,
Nor severed be, nor fall
From God, through ills that to this world belong.
To Thee, O Father Blessèd, I will sing,
Who art of this great universe the glorious King.

IV. (28–37).

Hushed be the world, and still,
   While I my task fulfil,
And lift to Thee, Supreme, the hymn divine;
   And while my prayers I pour,
   Let all on earth adore!
For earth, and all her workmanship, is Thine.
   Let blustering winds their tumults cease,
And rustling trees and shrill-voiced birds be all at
      peace.

V. (38–48).

   Let ether listener be
   To holy psalmody:
Let air be silent too: and rapid streams
   Adown the earth that pour,
   And waves that lash the shore,
Let all be stayed, as it in prayer beseems.
   And demon foes to holy strain,
Who haunt recesses dark, and in the tombs remain;

VI. (49–59).

Fly they—far, far away—
    While I my offerings pay:
But all the good, throughout creation's range,
    The happy ones who serve,
    Nor from the precepts swerve
Of the Great Parent, now in interchange
   Of holy thought and mind may they
Befriend, and upward these my hymns and prayers
    convey!

VII. (60–67).

The One, the only One,
    The Father Thou alone.
The One beginning whence all else began;
    The Fount whence all founts flow,
    The Root whence all roots grow;
The Good whence good in all its channels ran;
   The Star that to all stars gave birth;
The World whence sprang all worlds from highest
    heaven to earth.

VIII. (68–79).

The Form of all forms known:
All beauty is Thine own:
The hidden Seed, the ages' Parent Prop:
    Of worlds intelligent
    The Father, whence forth sent
Ambrosial Breath, and floating drop by drop
    Upon embodied bulk, combines
A second world, which in reflected glory shines.

IX. (80–88).

O Blessèd, Thee I praise,
    Or whether voice I raise,
Or solemn silence keep; for to Thine ear
    Not more the uttered speech
    Than Mind's still voice doth reach:
Unuttered though the word, yet Thou dost hear.
    With Thee I praise the First-born One,
The First-sprung Light, Thine own Begotten only
    Son.

x. (89–95).

Thou Lord of power and might,
Light of the Father light,
Of the Ineffable the glorious Word;
With the great Father Thee
I hymn in unity;
And Holy Spirit too in blest accord,
Who did Himself divinely spring
Forth from the Father and through Thee, with Thee I sing.

xi. (96–109).

True counsel He unfolds,
And middle rule [1] He holds:
Breath holy! Spur of Father, Spur of Son!
Self-Parent, and Self-Kin,
Self-nurtured Root within,
The Uncreated, Unbegotten One.
The Eternal glory is out-poured
Upon the Son: through whom forth springs the Spirit Lord.

---

[1] Middle Rule. See note on line 57, Ode V.

XII. (110–124).

God and of God is He,
    Mid light in Trinity.
Thee Trinity and Unity we name;
    For Thou art Three, yet One,
    The Father, Spirit, Son:
Though severed, yet unsevered, One the same.
    Forth went the Son to do Thy will,
And yet with Thee the Father He remaineth still.

XIII. (125–135).

Thy rule to bear He goes,
    And upon worlds bestows,
Whence He Himself received, life's happy store.
    The Word! to Thee I raise
    With the Great Father, praise.
The Mind of the Ineffable, before
    All worlds, did Thee beget; and Thou
Begotten art the Father's Word, to whom all bow!

XIV. (136-146).

Thou first from the first Root
Didst spring, the glorious Shoot;
And since Thy birth all things have birth from Thee.
The Eternal One, the Seed
Of all things, so decreed,
That Thou, first-sown, the Seed of all shouldst be.
For Thou dost all in all fulfil;
And 'tis by Thee that nature lived and liveth still:

XV. (147-159).

Where she is highest seen,
Where in the ranks between,
Where lowest: all good gifts of quickening powers
From God the Father she
Doth taste and hold through Thee.
Guided by Thee, this ageless sphere of ours
Turns her strong wheels on easy poles,
And seventh in the dance of stars unwearied rolls.

XVI. (160-170).

The many lights on high
    One surface beautify
In Thy great world: for Thou dost so ordain:
    And Thou, God's glorious Son,
    Didst make the ages run,
And in unbroken course dost them sustain.
    All in this globe Thou dost survey,
And all in circuit tend; and all Thy laws obey.

XVII. (171-180).

And in the depths of sky
    Unfathomed we descry
Thy ruling hand and power; for it is there
    That Thou the stars dost lead,
    And in Light's pastures feed
The glittering host, with a true Shepherd's care.
    To all in heaven, in earth, below,
Thou dost their tasks assign, and life on all bestow.

XVIII. (181–192).

To gods and mortal kind,
Whoe'er have quaffed of mind,
By kindly fate, the intellectual shower,
Thou Lord and Steward art:
And soul Thou dost impart
To those whose life hath nought but soul for dower,
And nature's unrestrained control:
For hangs on Thee the growth of even eyeless soul.

XIX. (193–212).

And things that lack Thy breath
Are yet upheld from death;
For Thou hast linked them to the One Supreme:
Whence flows to earth by Thee
Life's channel still kept free
Through trackless worlds; and the descending stream
Of good doth mould this world of ours
To form of unseen world of highest mental powers.

XX. (213–226).

A second sun hath shone
This lower world upon:
Parent of later light: and bright-eyed lord
Of what doth live to-day,
To-morrow to decay,
Base matter: he doth yet to us afford
All world-born good, by Thy decree;
And is, O Thou God-born, type visible of Thee.

XXI. (227–237).

Beyond mind's utmost reach,
Beyond all power of speech,
Ineffable, unknown, O Father dread!
Thou art of mind the Mind,
Of souls the Soul combined,
Of natures all Thou art the Fountain-head.
Behold! Thy servant bends the knee,
And down on earth a poor blind suppliant falls to Thee.

XXII. (238–251).

But Thou the light dost give,
    The light for mind to live;
To suppliant soul, O Blessèd, pity show:
    Diseases chase away,
    And cares the soul which slay,
And shameless earthly dog, and fiendish foe:
    Far from my soul and from my prayer,
Far from my life and deeds, chase every hurtful snare.

XXIII. (252–259).

Armed may my body be
    Against the enemy,
And armed my spirit, and whate'er is mine;
    Nor may he entrance find
    Within my heart or mind.
Out be he cast, and out, by help Divine,
    Remain, and leave me, and take flight,
The worldly fiend, who gives to passions strength and
        might.

XXIV. (260-274).

And who obstructs the road
Which upward leads to God;
And quencheth aspiration's holy flame.
But, O great King, give me,
Companion meet to be,
An angel of Thine own, of holy name,
Of holy aid, an angel friend,
Who may God-lighted prayer, and all good deeds defend.

XXV. (275-280).

A guardian may he be
Of soul and life to me,
And to my prayer and deeds protection yield;
My body may he save
From trouble's rushing wave,
And sickness; and from harm my spirit shield;
And o'er my soul oblivion pour
Of earthly passions which disturbed my peace before.

XXVI. (281-290).

So may I spend my life
All calm and free from strife!
So may my soul, in hymning Thy high praise,
Mount up with strengthened wing
From earth, and heavenward spring!
So may I cleanse from worldliness my ways,
Till I, set free from earth-bound chain,
No longer subject am to Fate's imperious reign;

XXVII. (291-299).

But gain those halls above,
And Thy blest folds of love,
Whence forth doth flow the fountain of the soul!
But Thou propitious be,
And helping hand give me!
Call me, O Blessèd! all my ways control!
Hear Thou Thy humble suppliant's cry,
And lift my soul from earth to native realms on high!

Synesius.

V.

Ὑμνῶμεν κοῦρον νύμφας,

(Tetrapod: spondaic: catalect.)

Awake, our lute, the child to sing
    Of bride unwedded, holy maid;
True Son of the Eternal King,
    Ere earth's foundations yet were laid.

Ineffable Thy counsels, Lord,
    Father of all, by which was born
The Christ! a virgin's throes afford
    The Light of Life to world forlorn!

A Man! and yet of ages gone,
    And of all ages yet to come,
Throughout eternity, the One
    Upholder, Perfecter, and Sum.

Thyself, O Christ, art Fount of Light,
   Light of the Father's Light, bright Ray!
Dark matter thou didst burst; and night
   To holy souls Thou turn'st to day.   16

Yea! Founder of the world Thou art,
   And moulder of each starry sphere:
To earth her spurs Thou dost impart;
   While men hail Thee their Saviour dear.   20

For Thee his chariot Titan drives,
   The quenchless fount of morning light.
From Thee the bull-faced moon derives
   Her power to loose the gloom of night.   24

By Thee the year with fruit is crowned:
   By Thee the flocks and herds are fed:
Productive Thou dost make the ground;
   And to the poor Thou givest bread.   28

For Thou from Thine o'erflowing store
   Of grace ineffable and love,
O'er surface of all worlds dost pour
   The fertile sunshine from above.   32

And from Thy bosom forth did spring
    To life both light, and mind, and soul:
O pity then Thine own offspring
    Imprisoned under hard control,   36

By mortal limbs, by flesh and blood,
    Coerced, and measures stern of fate:
O save Thine own, Thou great and good,
    Nor let sick mind sick body hate!   40

Persuasion to my words nod Thou,
    And to my deeds such honest fame,
That truth I never disavow,
    Nor Sparta[1] nor Cyrene shame!   44

But may my soul, unbowed by grief,
    Draw all her nourishment from Thee,
Stretching both eyes, in calm relief,
    Up to Thy light, from sorrow free!   48

That, cleansed from dregs of worldly soil,
    I may by straight course upward mount,
And 'scaping from earth's care and toil,
    Be mingled with the soul's own fount!   52

---

[1] Synesius was a native of Cyrene, which was an ancient colony of Sparta.

Life such of pure content and praise,
    Do Thou to Thy poor harper grant,
While still to Thee the hymn I raise,
    And glory to the Father chant,   56

And Spirit,[1] mid-enthroned compeer,
    The Parent Root and Branch between!
Be such on earth my bright career,
    Nor sin nor sorrow intervene;   60

Until, within the courts above,
    The travail of my soul shall cease,
Still singing hymns of heavenly love
    In glory and in perfect peace.   64

Thee, Thee, the Fount of love, we bless,
    O Father, rock and strength of Thine;
And Thee alike, His form express,
    And seal, all beauty, Son Divine;   68

---

[1] Here, as elsewhere, Synesius represents the Holy Spirit as seated between the Father and the Son, or holding the middle rank; cf. Ode III. l. 220; Ode IV. l. 97, in which latter place, as if to mend Synesius' theology, some sciolist has made additions contrary to the context, which additions I follow the learned editors in rejecting. In the New Testament the sacred order given in Matt. xxviii. 19, is not strictly or always followed; e. g. 2 Cor. xiii. 14, 1 Pet. i. 2, Rev. i. 4, 5. May this help to explain the difficult passage Heb. xii. 23, 24?

And Holy Breath, of both the crown,
   Whose quickening gifts like billows roll :
Thou with the Father, send Him down
   To cheer and fertilize my soul!

Synesius.

VI.[1]

Μετὰ παγᾶς ἁγίας αὐτολοχεύτοι

(*Trimeter ionic.*)

THEE, with the holy self-sprung Fount, we sing,
Who art from all eternity great King,
God and of God, immortal, glorious One,
The only Father's true and only Son!
To Thee, with Him, our praises all belong;
Thee will we crown with choicest flowers of song.
Son of the Father, Thou by birth Divine!
In Thee all bright the Father's glories shine.
And from the Father and through Thee, behold!
The spirit issues—mystery threefold! 10
And takes the middle place [1] of light and mind,
In Trinity and Unity combined.

[1] See note on Ode V. l. 57.

Poured was the sacred Fountain into Thee;
Yet One it was, and is eternally.
The Father's Wisdom, Mind, and beauteous Ray,
Eternal Son, Thou dost to all display.
Of hidden Deity the outstanding light,
In Thee the purposes Divine are bright;
For thus the Eternal Father did decree,
That Thou Beginning to all worlds shouldst be; 20
And bring to bodies shape and form combined
With powers, from highest source, of thought and
    mind.
The orb of heaven in wisdom Thou dost guide,
And shepherd o'er the flock of stars preside.
Thou leader art of angels' choir and band;
Thou dost the phalanx of God's hosts command.
And Thou too dost the mortal race befriend,
And all their paths and wandering steps attend.
The Spirit undivided Thou dost spread
O'er earth, and gather back to fountain-head 30
Thy gifts unwasted; for Thou dost unchain
Death's captives, bringing them to life again.
Accept, my King, this wreath of hymns from me;
And O! propitious to Thy servant be!

Grant Thou calm life : and stay the wandering tide,
And bid the flood through worldly straits subside;
From soul and limbs diseases dire repel ;
And all pernicious rush of passions quell.
Or wealth or poverty extreme forefend ;
And to just deeds fame honourable send.   40
Among the people good report accord ;
And with persuasion crown the gentle word ;
That waveless thus my mind may reap repose,
And I ne'er groan oppressed with earth's dark woes ;
But watered from thy heavenly-flowing rill,
My mind I may with wisdom's produce fill.

Synesius.

VII.

Πρῶτος νόμον εὑρόμαι

(Logaœdic.)

I FIRST invented in Thy praise,
O Blessèd, these new metric lays.
Immortal Thou ! of virgin mild
The holy ever glorious Child :
Hope of the world, salvation's stem,
O Jesus of Jerusalem !
To Thee I raise the song on high ;
To Thee my harp-strings joyful ply.
O show me favour, heavenly King !
Accept the music which I bring   10
Of holy melodies ; for Thou
Art He to whom my soul doth bow,

God over all, God's mighty Son,
The ever blest Immortal One !
The Eternal Father gave Thee birth ;
Birth Thou hast given to heaven and earth.
All worlds are Thine ; all nature Thine ;
And wisdom infinite, divine.
In heaven, as God, Thy fame is spread ;
Below, as mingled with the dead.   20
But when the blessèd day had shone
That Thou shouldst mortal flesh put on
Of virgin mother, then the star,
Seen by the magi from afar
In eastern clime, perplexed their mind
And varied skill ; nor could they find
Or who, or what, the child might be,
Or what the hidden deity ;
No answer could their wisdom bring ;
Or God, or doomed to die, or king.   30
'Tis well ! meet be your offerings :
Bring myrrh for death's last sufferings :
Bring royal presents of fine gold ;
And gifts of frankincense unfold.
My God ! here frankincense behold !
My King ! deign to receive the gold !

And O! Thou Saviour born to die,
Myrrh for Thy tomb let me supply!
And cleansèd was the earth by Thee,
And cleansèd were the waves of sea ; 40
And all the paths which upward bear,
In slender element of air ;
And dark recesses underground,
In succour to the dead there bound,
By Thee, great Conqueror, were trod;
And Hades stood aghast at God.
But O! propitious be, great King !
Smile on the tribute which I bring
Of tuneful songs and measured lays
Designèd for Thy holy praise. 50

Synesius.

VIII.

Ὑπὸ δώριον ἁρμογὰν

(*Logaœdic.*)

O! 'tis no theme of common things
That wakes my ivory-fastened strings!
To Thee, in solemn Dorian [1] strain,
I lift my heart and voice amain,
O blessèd, O Immortal One,
The holy Virgin's glorious Son!
But, O great King, save Thou my life
From cares and woes and worldly strife,
That from calamity all free
Both night and day I may praise Thee.   10
And to my mind mayst Thou convey
From mind's own fount, a clear bright ray.

---

[1] He uses the epithet *Dorian* in a general sense, to express that which is grave and sublime.

Unto my youth mayst Thou impart
Soundness of limbs and manly heart:
And may my deeds reflect Thy light
In honour, truth, and glory bright.
And on the ripeness of mine age
Mayst Thou the wisdom of the sage
Bestow, with health, the blessed mead
Of harvest rich from well-sown seed. 20
And on that darling son of mine
May Thy preserving mercy shine,
Whom, when just passing gate of death,
Thou didst restore to vital breath.
O Lord of life, 'twas Thou didst wrench
From Death's firm grasp, his prey, and quench
My burning grief in floods of joy;
For Thou didst give me back my boy;
And tears, O Father, Thou didst dry,
In answer to Thy suppliant's cry! 30
May son and daughter, much loved pair,
Thy kind protection ever share,
And all my house, in happy calm,
Be sheltered by Thine hand from harm!
And, O my Saviour King, bless Thou
The partner of my wedded vow;

From sickness and from sorrow free,
Faithful, one-minded, may she be,
Preserved by Thee from thought of sin,
All bright without, all pure within! 40
Untouched by roving passions' tide,
My honoured wife, my love, my pride!
Loose Thou my soul from baneful chains
Of worldly life, its cares and pains,
And floods of dismal grief and woe,
Which overwhelm this earth below.
O! thus prepared may I be found
With holy worshippers around
To lead the choir, and chants to raise
To Thy all-glorious Father's praise; 50
And to Thy majesty, great King,
Loud hymns again I hope to sing;
Again in voice of praise Thy name
To bless, Thy honours to proclaim;
May be, my harp I shall again
Tune all-unhurt to highest strain.

Synesius.

IX.

Πολυήρατε, κύδιμε,

(*Logaœdic.*)

To THEE, much loved, be honour paid,
O glorious Child of Hebrew maid!
To Thee I raise the hymn anew,
Who didst the serpent's wiles subdue,
And drive afar the infernal foe
That filled e'en Paradise with woe:
For, subtle with forbidden fruit,
Of woeful knowledge nurse and root,
Our primal founder he o'ercame,
And smote the world with death and shame.   10
All-glorious Thou with many a crown!
Thou didst to wretched earth come down,
To dwell with man by death assailed,
Thyself in mortal body veiled;

And Thou dark Tartarus didst tread,
Midst countless nations of the dead.
Then Hades, ancient-born, amazed,
Did shudder as on Thee he gazed;
And the all-devouring savage hound [1]
Backward recoiled with frightened bound.   20
But lo! to holy souls, oppressed
With direful woes, Thou gavest rest,
That they in chorus led by Thee,
To praise the Father might be free.
And from below when Thou didst rise,
The demon-hosts beneath the skies,
Unnumbered, quaked, O mighty King,
To hear the judgment Thou shouldst bring.
Then did the stars, immortal band,
Gazing at Thee, astonished stand.   30
But Ether laughed, the father he—
The father wise—of harmony;
And mingled from his seven-toned lyre
Bright notes of music's holy fire,
Raising to Lord of earth and sky,
The song of victory on high.

---

[1] The fabled Cerberus, *Janitor Orci*.

And Lucifer, the guide of day,
With smiling countenance was gay;
And golden Hesperus afar
Shot beams, the Cythereïan star.　　　40
And shepherdess of night, the Moon
Filled her bright crescent with festoon,
And flowering wreath of liquid fire,
And led her peers in joyous choir.
And through the trackless paths of air
Titan spread out his flaming hair:
For God's own Son, the master Mind
Which did all things create and bind
In mutual law, full well he knew,
From whom his primal fire he drew.　　　50
But Thou, as plying heavenly oar,
Or wing of bird, didst upward soar
With holy feet; and o'er the skies
And dark-blue-vaulted heaven didst rise,
Up-mounting to the spheres of light,
The realms of Mind for ever bright.
There goodness from the Fountain-head
In bliss through silent heaven is spread;
There nor deep-flowing restless Time
Drags earthborn children through the slime　　　60

Of coarser matter, nor hard fates
Roll turbid floods o'er mortal states;
But Age himself, the ancient-sprung,
Is ageless, old at once, and young;
And in the unfading courts of love
Is steward to the blest above.

Synesius.

X.[1]

Μνώεο Χριστὲ,

(*Anapæstic monometer.*)

1.

LORD JESU, think on me;
    And this poor offering,
Which I do humbly weave for Thee,
    Accept, O Christ, my King.

2.

Lord Jesu, think on me,
    And purge away my sin:
From earthborn passions set me free,
    And make me pure within.

---

[1] In translating this ode I have given my spirit more liberty. It may be considered as a paraphrase or amplification, rather than an exact translation of the original. A brief form of it appears in *Hymns Ancient and Modern*.

3.

Lord Jesu, think on me,
  With care and woe oppressed;
Let me Thy loving servant be,
  And taste Thy promised rest.

4.

Lord Jesu, think on me
  Amid the battle's strife:
In all my pain and misery
  Be Thou my Health and Life.

5.

Lord Jesu, think on me,
  Nor let me go astray:
Through darkness and perplexity
  Point Thou the heavenly way.

6.

Lord Jesu, think on me,
  When flows the tempest high:
When on doth rush the enemy,
  O Saviour, be Thou nigh.

7.

Lord Jesu, think on me,
    That when the flood is past,
I may the Eternal Brightness see,
    And share Thy joy at last.

8.

Lord Jesu, think on me,
    And grant me my desire,
That I, with mind and limbs set free,
    May join the heavenly choir.

9.

Lord Jesu, think on me,
    That I may sing above
Praise to the Father, and to Thee,
    And to the Holy Dove.

GREGORY

BISHOP OF NAZIANZUS

(Born A.D. 325. Died, 389).

THIS eminent man needs no introduction from my humble pen. His praises are, and always have been, in the Church. Born near Nazianzus in Cappadocia, he succeeded his father in that episcopate. He cultivated his natural gifts, and increased his learning, at Athens. Thence he went forth to be a champion of the Christian faith, and a luminary in the great Church constellation of the fourth century. After the deliverance from the last effort of paganism contrived and led by the Emperor Julian, who had once been his friend and fellow-collegian, he displayed his great talents and eloquence at Constantinople, of which great Eastern capital for a time he became bishop. But soon he retired to the solitary cell, which he had before loved and frequented, near his native place, Nazianzus; and there renewed and exercised his gift of sacred poetry, of which, to name but one, his Hymn to God is an undying record, and may bear comparison with any similar composition in any age.

Gregory Nazianzen.

I.

HYMN TO CHRIST.

Σὲ τὸν ἄφθιτον μονάρχην

(*Dimeter ionicus.*)

1.

O THOU, the One Supreme,
   O Thou, the deathless King,
Be Thou my only theme:
   Grant me Thyself to sing.
To Thee the hymn, to Thee the praise,
Celestial choirs for ever raise.

2.

For Thee the ages run
   In order as was given;
For Thee shines forth the sun,
   The day-born eye of heaven:
For Thee the moon, and grand array
Of stars, hold on their nightly way.

3.

With reasonable soul
    For Thee learns favoured man
His passions to control,
    And the Divine to scan;
For Thou of all Creator art,
Thou mad'st the whole and every part.

4.

All march in ordered band:
    O'er all Thou hold'st the reins:
All creatures of Thy hand
    Thy Providence sustains.
For Thou the word didst speak—'twas done—
That Word of Thine is God the Son.

5.

For of same honour He,
    Thine own begotten Son,
In form and quality
    With Thee the Father one:
Who placed all things in harmony,
That over all He King might be.

6.

And all Thy works infolding
  In bonds of love and truth,
The Spirit all-upholding
  Renews creation's youth :
Foreseeing, He for all provides,
And Guardian over all presides.

7.

Thee, Thee, the Triune King,
  The One Eternal Lord,
Thee evermore I'll sing,
  By earth and heaven adored,
The Three in One, the One in Three,
The ever-living Trinity.

8.

Immovable of mind,
  Of ways past mortal ken,
The boundless, undefined,
  Wisdom's deep origin,
Upholder of the heavenly towers,
Ruler of all created powers.

9.

Beginning none, nor end:
   The self-sprung Light art Thou:
We cannot comprehend,
   But to Thy Brightness bow,
Whose eye, repelling mortal gaze,
All things above, below, surveys.

10.

Unseen, yet ever near,
   Father, propitious be:
This my petition hear,
   This boon accord to me:
That Light to serve through endless day,
And have my sins all washed away;

11.

That I, with conscience clear
   From every evil thought,
May love with filial fear,
   And worship as I ought,
Pure holy hands and heart upraising,
And Christ the Lord for ever praising.

12.

To Thee I bend the knee;
　When He shall come, grant me,
That I His glory see,
　That I His servant be:
When He shall come—shall come again;
When He shall come—shall come to reign.

13.

Father, propitious be!
　On me Thy mercy show!
Bow down Thine ear to me,
　On me Thy grace bestow;
For Thine the glory, Thine the grace,
While countless ages run their race.

II.

HYMN TO GOD.

'Ω πάντων ἐπέκεινα· τί γὰρ θέμις ἄλλο σε μέλπειν;

(*Dactylic hexameter.*)

1.

O Thou, the One Supreme o'er all![1]
    For by what other name
May we upon Thy greatness call,
    Or celebrate Thy fame?

2.

Ineffable! to Thee what speech
    Can hymns of honour raise?
Ineffable! what tongue can reach
    The measure of Thy praise?

---

[1] Or, O Thou beyond the range of all—πάντων ἐπέκεινα.

3.

How, unapproached, shall mind of man
    Descry Thy dazzling throne;
And pierce, and find Thee out, and scan,
    Where Thou dost dwell alone?

4.

Unuttered Thou! all uttered things
    Have had their birth from Thee:
The One unknown! from Thee the springs
    Of all we know and see!

5.

Mindful, and mindless, all things yield
    To Thy parental sway
For Thou to all art life and shield:
    They honour and obey.

6.

For round Thee centre all the woes
    Of night and darkling day,
The common wants and common throes;
    And all to Thee do pray.

7.

And all things as they move along
  In order fixed by Thee,
Thy watchword heed, in silent song
  Hymning Thy majesty.

8.

And lo! all things abide in Thee,
  And through the complex whole,
Thou spread'st Thine own Divinity,
  Thyself of all the goal.

9.

One Being Thou, all things, yet none,
  Nor one nor yet all things;
How call Thee, O mysterious One?
  A worthy name who brings?

10.

All-named from attributes Thine own,
  How call Thee as we ought?
Thou art unlimited, alone,
  Beyond the range of thought.

11.

What heaven-born intellect shall rend
   The veiling clouds above?
Be Thou propitious! ever send
   Bright tokens of Thy love!

12.

O Thou the One Supreme o'er all!
   For by what other name
May we upon Thy greatness call,
   Or celebrate Thy fame?

III.

HYMN TO CHRIST ON EASTER DAY
(AFTER LONG SILENCE),

Χριστὲ ἄναξ, σὲ πρῶτον, ἐπεὶ λόγον ἠέρι δῶκα,
δηναιὸν κατέχων, φθέγξομ' ἀπὸ στομάτων,

(*Dactylic hexameter, and pentameter.*)

O CHRIST the King! since breath pent up so long
I have outpoured, Thou first shalt be my song;
May this my word, the current of my mind,
If lawful thus to speak, acceptance find,
And unto Thee as holy incense rise
Of holiest priest, a grateful sacrifice!
The Father's Brightness, Word of the Great Mind,
Who cannot be by power of speech defined,
High Light of highest Light, the Only Son,
Image and Seal of the Immortal One,   10
Without beginning; from same Fount of Light
With the Great Spirit; infinite in might:

All-glorious Thou, and Author of all good :
From age to age Thy truth hath firmly stood.
Enthroned Thou reignest high in heaven above,
Almighty Breath of Mind and Lord of Love.
Throughout this framèd universe Divine
Whatever is, or shall be, all is Thine :
Thou madest all, to all Thou givest life,
And all Thou guidest : nowhere fault or strife,   20
Nor error in Thy workmanship is found :
The whole in willing chain to Thee is bound.
Thou laid'st the world's foundation : and Thy nod
All things obey, and own their Sovereign God.
For Thee the lofty sun, the king of day,
Quenching the stars, holds on his fiery way.
For Thee, for so Thou bidst, the eye of night,
The moon, waxes and wanes, full orb of light.
For Thee the belt of heaven, all-dancing ring,
And seasons kindly mingling, laugh and sing.   30
For Thee the fixèd stars and planets shine
In course, and speak Thy wisdom all divine.
Thy light they are, the heavenly minds that be,
All sing on high the glorious Trinity.
Man is Thy glory too, angel below,
Here placed to sing, O Light, Thy beauteous glow.

Immortal, fleshless, glory's highest ray,
Who mortal flesh yet took'st, man's woes to stay,
For Thee I live, for Thee my songs arise,
For Thee I am a breathing sacrifice;   40
For this, of all things once possessed by me,
Alone remains, and this I give to Thee.

I tie my tongue, and loose it at Thy will;
In either, what Thou wouldst may I fulfil,
Speak what is right, nor think aught else beside:
From mire select the pearl, with Thee my Guide;
Gold from the sand, the rose from thorny brake,
From straw-encumbered ears the pure grain take.

To Thee, O Christ, this wreath of uttered praise,
As firstfruits of my loving toil, I raise.   50

For from the dead, with whom He mingled lay,
Great Christ arose, upon this gladsome day;
Gates of grim Hades He did open fling;
And broke death's power, and robbed him of his sting;
Rushed from the tomb, appeared to speaking men,
For whom, once born, He died and rose again;
That we new-born might rise, from death set free,
And ever live, ascending Lord, with Thee.

This day glad Heaven with acclamation rings,
And choir angelic crowning anthem sings.   60
This day my closèd lips I loose in song
To Thee, to whom my lute and breath belong.

Of mind to Mind, of word to the true Word,
I here have offered what I could afford:
Hereafter, if He will, I hope to bring
To the Great Spirit worthier offering.

IV.

"TO HIS OWN SOUL."[1]

τί σοι θέλεις γενέσθαι;

(*Iambic dimeter catalectic.*)

1.

O SOUL of mine, repining,
   What wouldst have done for thee?
Speak, great or small defining:
   Granted thy wish shall be.

2.

Of all bright things, prized highest,
   Beneath the rolling sun,
Tell that for which thou sighest;
   For thee it shall be done.

---

[1] The original is one of the most spirited pieces anywhere to be found, truly forcible and racy.

3.

Wouldst thou assume the measure
 Of Gyges, Lydia's king,
To hide or show at pleasure
 By power of magic ring?

4.

Wouldst thou rich Midas follow?
 " All gold I touch," he cried:
'Tis given! e'en gold to swallow:
 So all of gold he died.

5.

Wouldst shine in brilliant trammels,
 With pearls and jewels grand?
Have flocks, and herds, and camels,
 And acres of fat land?

6.

Such things we will not barter:
 To thee they were a snare:
They are not in our charter,
 Nor would I have them there.

7.

For since to God advancing
  I came at His own call,
Such cares the soul entrancing,
  I have abandoned all.

8.

Wouldst have the nations bending
  Beneath thy yoke to day,
To-morrow thyself lending
  To grace another's sway?

9.

The sway of one, once marching,
  It might be, at thy side;
Or menial base, now arching
  His neck in lofty pride?

10.

Wouldst thou in Love's sweet anguish,
  In indolence and ease,
Let truth and honour languish,
  And change with changing breeze?

11.

Wouldst wed a fair Heth's daughter,
  Fair progeny to see?
Ah me! of woes and slaughter
  Progenitor to be!

12.

Wouldst have the commons sounding
  The greatness of thy fame,
And theatres rebounding
  With echoes of thy name?

13.

Wouldst thou in courts o'erflowing
  With legal mockery,
Justice and truth o'erthrowing,
  Pillage, and pillaged be?

14.

Wouldst take a martial bearing,
  And sport with blood and gore?
Or, Pythian garlands wearing,
  Defy the lion's roar?

15.

Wouldst have the town applauding,
    And statues reared to thee?
The world thy merits lauding,
    Wouldst thou its idol be?

16.

Vain wish! a shadowy dreaming,
    A moan of wind hence bound,
Whiz of an arrow gleaming,
    A hand-clap's dying sound.

17.

Such things will fade to-morrow,
    However bright to-day:
And he must sleep in sorrow
    Who makes them his heart's stay.

18.

Toys common! bad men's heaven!
    And ah! when hence they go,
To none is it then given
    To carry aught below.

19.

What then, O soul repining,
   Since these things nothing be,
Substantial good defining,
   'Wouldst thou have done for thee?

20.

Wouldst be a god, presiding
   At God's own side most high,
Angelic chorus guiding,
   All radiant o'er the sky?

21.

Go thou, on pinions gliding
   Of vehement desire,
On rapid whirlwind riding
   Whither thou dost aspire.

22.

To plume thy wing I'm trying,
   Nor spare the friendly goad:
Mount upward, bird-like flying
   On thine ethereal road.

23.

But earth's own child on crutches,
    Since I am yoked to thee,
As queen in butchers' clutches,
    Just tell how this must be;

24.

Whom wilt thou have abettor,
    To be upheld in breath?
For I'm no more thy debtor,
    Nor heed vain threats of death.

25.

Or wouldst thou perfumed table,
    With dainties covered o'er,
So art cuisine be able
    To stimulate thee more?

26.

And lyre, and whirl so maddening
    Of rapid foot and hand,
And things to tell too saddening,
    Known to the revelling band?

27.

Art thou for such things wrangling?
  Have thy desire!—but wait:
Such things, not life, but strangling,
  To friends insatiate!

28.

For thee a house abideth,
  A rock with self-formed dome;
Nature herself provideth:
  We give thee such a home!

29.

Or if thy fancy leadeth
  To build thyself a cell,
But little toil it needeth,
  Where thou mayst safely dwell.

30.

The body claims small payment,
  Ere it returns to dust:
Skins, camel's hair, for raiment
  Sufficed of old the just.

31.

And grass, or straw, as chances,
    Make thou thy humble bed :
And purple heath, or branches,
    Thy coverlet be spread.

32.

Such for my guests is meetest :
    No fear to great or small :
Plain table : odours sweetest,
    Kind earth's free gifts to all.

33.

Thus housed, we will thee nourish,
    As best we can afford :
Wouldst eat? take bread and flourish :
    Take meal, if on the board.

34.

Here's salt : and thyme we scant not :
    Such source no toil requires :
More luxuries we want not,
    Whate'er the world desires.

35.

Or drink wouldst thou? there springeth
    An everflowing bowl:
No bane the fountain bringeth,
    Bright cheerer of the soul.

36.

But wouldst unbend in season,
    And not, o'erstrained, repine?
We grant in this is reason,
    Nor grudge the rough-made wine.

37.

But thou dost spurn all measure,
    And wouldst the vessel bore,
And take huge draughts of pleasure
    Till thou couldst hold no more.

38.

Then seek another helot,
    All lengths with thee to go:
No idler I, nor zealot,
    To nurse domestic foe.

39.

A frozen reptile taken,
    And with fond warmth caressed:
See! it to life doth waken,
    And wound me in the breast.

40.

Wouldst boundless gold-roofed mansions,
    Gemmed paragons of art,
And master-piece expansions,
    To life which almost start?

41.

Colours with colours blending
    In opposite array;
Rare tablets, softness lending,
    Or shining bright as day?

42.

Dost long for robes wide-flowing,
    Pride of the untouched great;
And wealth on fingers glowing,
    Incredible to state?

43.

Art thou at beauty aiming?
　The wise would scorn to win:
More I than all, proclaiming
　That beauty is within.

44.

Thus I to men benighted,
　Of earth the creatures fond,
For time alone quick-sighted,
　With not a thought beyond.

45.

But ye who soar up higher,
　A noble life to live;
Who would to heaven be nigher,
　Behold what God doth give!

46.

In poorest clay there dwelleth
　That which can never die:
With this my bosom swelleth:
　For this I food supply!

47.

God-minded, thyself harden !
    Meet calm the flashing sword !
Plant trees for God's own garden !
    Be worker with the Lord !

48.

Up ! living words be building,
    In God's blest truth secure.
Not robbed by foe's false gilding
    Through pleasure's baneful lure !

49.

Again of life eternal,
    Approach the blessèd tree :
The way, O Thou Supernal,
    I've found in knowing Thee.

50.

Past, present, never-ending,
    The One great Light in Three ;
To whom all things are tending :
    To Thee all glory be !

EPILOGUE.

51.

To self the wise thus speaketh,
  Turning his eyes within;
And eager there he seeketh
  To find out lurking sin.

52.

But who to speak refuseth,
  Will pass his days in vain:
Nay, more! the ease he chooseth,
  May end in greatest pain.

V.

A MORNING PRAYER.

Ὄρθρος·[1] δίδωμι τῷ Θεῷ μου δεξιὰς,

(*Iambic trimeter.*)

'Tis dawn: to God I lift my hand,
  To regulate my way;
My passions rule, and unmoved stand,
  And give to Thee the day:

Not one dark word or deed of sin,
  Nor one base thought allow;
But watch all avenues within,
  And wholly keep my vow.

Shamed were my age, should I decline;
  Shamed were Thy table too,
At which I stand:—the will is mine:
  Give grace, my Christ, to do.

---

[1] Ὄρθριος violates metre; I would retain the reading ὄρθρος, and put a colon. Thus, as it seems to me, grammar, sense, and metre, may be all satisfied.

VI.

A HYMN AT NIGHT, AFTER FAILURE TO KEEP VOW.

ἐψευσάμην σε τὴν ἀλήθειαν, λόγε,

(*Iambic trimeter.*)

O Thou, the Word of truth divine!
   All light I have not been,
Nor kept the day as wholly Thine;
   For Thou dark spots hast seen.

The day is down: night hath prevailed:
   My Lord I have belied;
I vowed, and thought to do, but failed;
   My steps did somewhere slide.

There came a darkness from below
   Obscuring safety's way.
Thy light, O Christ, again bestow;
   Turn darkness into day.

VII.

AN EVENING HYMN.

Σὲ καὶ νῦν εὐλογοῦμεν,

(*Semi-iambic.*)

1.

AND now again at night,
 O Christ, the living Word,
Thou Light of the Eternal Light,
 Be Thou by us adored.

2.

Thou dost the Spirit give,
 Third Light, in glory one;
His grace, by whom alone we live,
 Thou dost refuse to none.

3.

Thou didst the darkness scatter,
   Thou mad'st the light to shine,
That now through all primeval matter
   Might spring delight divine.

4.

It, a rude mass before,
   From Thee took order new;
And shapely form, and steadfast law,
   So beautiful to view.

5.

And mind of man with light
   From heaven Thou didst endow,
By word and wisdom that he might
   Thine image bear below;

6.

And lighted in his soul,
   Thine own great Light might see;
And thenceforth not in part, but whole,
   Himself all light might be.

7.

And heaven Thou didst array,
 With those bright orbs above;
And day to night, and night to day,
 Proclaim Thy law of love;

8.

Yielding in turn; the one
 To worn-out flesh brings rest!
The other calls, "Let work be done!"
 Such work as Thou lov'st best.

VIII.

ADMONITORY ADDRESS TO A VIRGIN.[1]

Παρθένε, νύμφη Χριστοῦ,

(*The Greek is of varied metre, arranged in lines of generally seven syllables each.*)

    O BRIDE of Christ on high,
    Thy Bridegroom glorify!
    Always thyself keep pure,
    In word and wisdom sure,
    That bright with Him all-bright
    Thou e'er mayst dwell in light.
    Far better spouse is He
    Than earthly spouse could be :
    Thy union happier far
    Than mortal unions are.   10

---

[1] This poem, though lacking the spirit and vigour of the *Address to his own Soul*, may yet find acceptance with some; and though the times are utterly changed, and what in an age of pagan persecution "was good for the present distress" (1 Cor. vii. 26) may be so no longer, yet there is much in it of good instruction : the style is pretty and occasionally elevated.

In bodily estate
Thou yet didst imitate
The intellectual powers,
Giving to Him thy hours:
And didst acquire on earth
The angels' right of birth.
'Tis "bind and loose" below,
Bodies from bodies grow:
Above each stands alone,
Nor loosing *there* is known.   20

Of pure existence, they
First bear the ethereal ray,
Spirit and fire: none rests,
Doing great God's behests.
But now wild matter found—
All nature flowing round
With unresisted force—
A mingled intercourse;
But God the flood restrained,
And marriage laws ordained.   30
But thou hast hence escaped,
And upward thy course shaped;
From matter's base alloy
To spirit's holy joy.

Mind harmonized with mind,
Doth truest pleasure find:
Such harmony is thine,
A harmony divine.
With flesh thou war dost wage,
And helpest God's image: 40
For thou art God's own breath,
With body yoked till death:
That out of wrestling sore,
At length the battle o'er,
And earth well beaten down,
Thou mayst receive the crown.
To marriage also raise,
But only second praise.
That is for passion given,
This is bright light of heaven: 50
That founds a pure offspring,
This is self-offering.
This honoured was, we hold,
At seasons marked of old.
To this in Paradise
Lo! Adam testifies:
For this on Sinai's peak
Doth Moses also speak;

And Zachary the priest,
Of God's true saints not least, 60
And whom we hail the rather
As the Forerunner's father.
But marriage hath its need:
Hence springs a holy seed:
And hence the virgin[1] bride,
Honoured at God's own side.
Yet of the flesh it is, and earth,
All earthly from its birth.
When law and shadows ruled,
And we were sometime schooled, 70
Marriage held sceptre mild,
Yet like a little child.
But when the letter died,
The Spirit was supplied:
For Christ had come and borne
In flesh our woes and scorn:
Had brought Redemption nigh,
And then ascended high:
Christ, sprung from Virgin's womb,
Christ, Conqueror o'er the tomb. 80

---

[1] Virgin bride—that is, the Church. So Methodius in his *Virgins' Song*, and all the early Christians. See Rev. xxi. 2, 9, etc.

Then continence did rise,
And this base world despise,
Which should its course have mended,
And high with Christ ascended.

Thou journey'st well! but haste!
Behind is fiery waste :
Take to thy steps good heed,
And to the mountain speed.
Cast not one backward glance
On Sodom, lest perchance
Thou, fixed upon the ground,
A pile of salt be found.
In battling with the flesh
Take ever courage fresh,
Neither by terror bent,
Nor over-confident.
Faint not, for He is nigh
Who will all strength supply.

A spark may kindle hell :
Water the flame doth quell.
Full means to thee are lent
For good self-government.

Let thou the fear of God
Freeze the rebellious blood:
Fasting the flesh control:
Keep watches o'er thy soul,
And pour it forth in prayer:
Such thy true weapons are.
Add tears: and lowly bed,
With reeds or rushes spread : 110
One constant flame of love
Rising to God above,
And lulling all desire
Which doth not up aspire.
The fallen rise by thee!
The shipwrecked pitied be!
Thyself live out the gale,
Expanding Hope's bright sail.

They fall not who ne'er rise,
But they who try the skies. 120
Few mount on pinion wings:
Straight course to humbler things.
Fell Lucifer through pride:
Angels in heaven reside.

One, traitor, sunk in night :
The eleven are stars of light.

Be pure, be wholly pure,
Of this make ever sure,
Lest thou, by heeding not,
Christ's spotless robe shouldst spot.
Let modest be thine eye :
Thy tongue speak maidenly :
Thy mind not pandering,
Thy foot not wandering :
Nor loud laugh marking thee,
As one we blush to see.

Thy poor and tarnished wear,
Thy unadornèd hair,
I honour more than pearls,
Or silken dress, or curls.

Fair flower is modest face,
And paleness is true grace :
And virtues plentiful
Are braid most beautiful.
With paints let others dress
The living God's likeness ;

Live tablet they of sin,
And all that's base within.
Whate'er thou hast of beauty,
Die let it all to duty : 150
But beauty of the soul—
'Tis God's—*it* keep thou whole.

Of men, though good they be,
The sight 'twere best thou flee.
Some cheat might thee entrance,
Or be entranced perchance :
Eye now with eye bespangling,
And word with word entangling,
Then cheek with cheek o'erglowing,
And mutual passion flowing. 160
'Tis well : but not for thee :
Not thine the accursed tree :
The tree of Life thy care :
The serpent's guile beware !

O maiden, hear my word,
Have thou no other lord ;
Thy Bridegroom reigns above,
And bids thee faithful prove.

Thou from the flesh hast fled,
And it to thee is dead.
Why turn to it again,
And make thy work all vain?
That singleness of thine
Is a rare gift divine:
Few they whom it adorns,
As rose among the thorns.
Such grace 'tis thine to know:
High o'er the snares below,
By which the wicked fall,
Thou safely passest all.

Lo! one no sooner builds,
And bridal chamber gilds,
Than *she* with mournful gloom
Forth bears him to the tomb.
Felt one a father's pride?
At once the loved child died.
And oh! the mother's pain
Of travailing in vain!

And jealousy, ah me!
How frightful 'tis to see,

When each the other taunts,
Where stolen friendship haunts!

What wormwood and what gall,
Worst recompence of all,
To rear up family,
And then dishonoured be!

One care is thine, one call,
To look to God in all!
But little thou dost need:
That little God will speed. 200

Shelter and barley cake
Sufficient wealth will make:
Nor shall dire need impart
Keen edge to tempter's dart,
As when Christ, hard bestead,
He bade turn stones to bread.

By thee, however tried,
Be all base gain denied:
Fowls of the air God feeds,
Sure then His saints He heeds. 210

Of oil, if faith prevail,
Thy cruse shall never fail.
By Cherith's desert brook
At the great Prophet look !
To feed him ravens sped :
So too shalt thou be fed !

How Thecla from the flame,[1]
And lions, unscathed came,
Thou know'st : and how great Paul,
Preacher of truth to all,   220
Bore hunger, thirst, and cold,
Through death's worst forms still bold ;
That thou might'st look, O maid,
To God alone for aid,
Who in the wilderness
With food can myriads bless.

Lo ! beauty fadeth fast,
Nor will earth's glories last :
Wealth is a failing stream,
And power an empty dream.   230

---

[1] Thecla, see *The Virgins' Song*, of Methodius, p. 141.

But thou, faith's sail unfurled,
Hast fled this erring world,
Steering thy course on high
To realms beyond the sky.
There in the holy shrine
Thou shalt for ever shine:
And there with angels raise
The song of endless praise!

A better portion far
Than sons and daughters are! 240

But maidens, be ye wise,
And watch with longing eyes,
That when Christ shall return
Your lamps may brightly burn:
That with the Bridegroom ye
May enter in, and see
The beauty and the grace
Of His own dwelling place,
And share in truth and love
The mysteries above. 250

PSALM OF THE NAASSENI.[1]

(THE AUTHOR UNKNOWN.)

Νόμος ἦν γενικὸς τοῦ παντὸς ὁ πρώτιστος νόος·

(Anapæstic logaœdic.)

THE first Eternal Mind was law to all,
And did the Universe to being call :
Next, of the First-born forth was chaos spread :
And thirdly, soul on task of labour sped :
But it in vesture thin, and slight array,
O'ercome with toil, to death becomes a prey.
At one time regnant it beholds the light ;
Then soon laments, cast down in piteous plight.
'Tis hazard all : now joy, now grief, befalls ;
And now it dies, and now fresh life recalls.

---

[1] For a full account of the Naasseni, who they were, and what were their opinions, I would refer the reader to *Hyppolytus, Antenicene Christian Library*, vol. i. book v. Suffice it here to say that they were a learned sect of Gnostics ; that they held very strange opinions ; but were great hymn makers. A translation of this particular Psalm may be found in the same volume, p. 153. I had made my translation before I was aware of this.

In never-ending labyrinth of woes
It, wretched, hither now, now hither goes.
Then Jesus spake : On earth, O Father, see
How things have strayed in dire perplexity
Far from Thy Breath : how floods of evil roll,
And in base matter overwhelm the soul !
Escape it seeks from bitter woe all round,
But knows not where a passage may be found.
O Father, Me upon this errand send :
Bearing Thy seals, I will the depths descend ;
Throughout whole ages I will make my way,
All mysteries of darkness turn to day ;
And godlike forms I thenceforth will display :
Forth Knowledge I will call to quell all strife,
And upward show the holy paths of life.

METHODIUS

BISHOP AND MARTYR

(Died about A.D. 311).

METHODIUS, a father of the Church, and a martyr, was Bishop of Olympas or Patara, in Lycia, and afterwards of Tyre in Palestine. He lived during the last half of the third century, and died a martyr at Chalcis in Greece, probably A.D. 311, during the Diocletian persecution. Jerome[1] ranks him among the popular writers, and commends him especially for the neatness of his style.[2]

This Virgins' Song of his composing is in twenty-four parts, or strophies, each beginning with a letter of the alphabet in order from A to Ω.[3] Ten virgins are

---

[1] *De Viris Illust.* c. 83.
[2] MOSHEIM, *Eccl. Hist.*, vol. i. pp. 236–7.
[3] Cf. Psalm cxlv., with the letters in order of the Hebrew alphabet. In Greek poetry many instances of the same thing occur. It was useful as an aid to the memory.

supposed to be present. Thecla[1] leads, giving the strophy in each case, the rest join in chorus, singing the burden or refrain (ἐφύμνιον). The learned editors refer to the Συμπόσιον of Plato, also to the Παρθένια of Alcman and Pindar; which Methodius may in part have imitated.

[1] See in Gregory's *Admonitory Address to a Virgin*, above, p. 125: also in the Anacreontic Ode of Sophronius, in which the praises and exploits of this first female martyr are set forth, pp. 32, 44–5, of the Greek *Anthology*.

THE VIRGINS' SONG.

Ἄνωθεν, παρθένοι, βοῆς ἐγερσίνεκρος ἦχος

(*Iambic metre, varied.*)

I.

THE Bridegroom cometh! overhead
The shout descending wakes the dead!
   Go forth to meet the King,
   The gates just entering!
Virgins, white-robed, with lamps haste eastward forth
     to meet Him,
   Haste ye, O haste to greet Him!

THE REFRAIN.

With holy feet, and lamps bright burning,
I go to meet my Lord returning.

2.

Earth's mournful bliss I left, and toys
Of wanton life, and foolish joys:
   To Thee alone I cling:
   Thou art my Life, my King:
Grant that I may, O Blessèd, ever close to Thee,
   Thy royal beauty see!

THE REFRAIN.

With holy feet, and lamps bright burning,
I go to meet my Lord returning.

3.

Thou art my wealth: for Thee I fled
All worldly lure; and upward sped;
   And come in spotless dress
   Of Thine own Righteousness,
With Thee to enter in the bridal chamber gates,
   Where perfect bliss awaits.

THE REFRAIN.

With holy feet, and lamps bright burning,
I go to meet my Lord returning.

4.

Saved from the dragon's myriad wiles,
By which the simple he beguiles,
   I bore the dreadful fire,
   And wild beasts' savage ire;
Waiting till Thou from Heaven, O Hope of all creation,
   Shouldst come to my salvation!

THE REFRAIN.

With holy feet, and lamps bright burning,
I go to meet my Lord returning.

5.

My home and country for Thy sake,
And maiden dance, I did forsake,
   And mother's pride and race,
   And thoughts of rank and place:
For Thou, O Christ the Word, art all in all to me:
   I long for naught save Thee!

THE REFRAIN.

With holy feet, and lamps bright burning,
I go to meet my Lord returning.

L

6.

Hail! Christ the Life, unchanging Day,
Accept this humble virgin lay:
   To Thee our song of praise
   With heart and voice we raise!
In Thee, O Thou perfection's flower, O Word Divine,
   Love, joy, mind, wisdom, shine.

THE REFRAIN.

With holy feet, and lamps bright burning,
I go to meet my Lord returning.

7.

O Bride, triumphant now in light,
And clad in robes of purest white,
   Sweet-breathing, sinless, free,
   Ope wide the gates to me:
Sit we in self-same company near Christ above,
   And sing thy marriage, Love!

THE REFRAIN.

With holy feet, and lamps bright burning,
I go to meet my Lord returning.

8.

Ah me! some virgins vainly pour
Their sobs and cries outside the door:
   Their lamps are quenched, and they
   No burning light display:
Their error they would mend: but ah! they come too late,
   And closèd is the gate.

THE REFRAIN.

With holy feet, and lamps bright burning,
I go to meet my Lord returning.

9.

For they a foolish part had played,
And from the sacred pathway strayed;
   Oil, they had purchased none:
   Ah! wretched and undone!
Forbidden with dead lamps the home of bliss to see.
   They wail their misery.

THE REFRAIN.

With holy feet, and lamps bright burning,
I go to meet my Lord returning.

10.

Lo! goblet filled with sweetest wine:
Drink we, O virgins, 'tis Divine;
   And forth-set for our need:
   Lo! this is drink indeed;
This for the guests, who to the marriage bidden are,
   The Bridegroom doth prepare.

THE REFRAIN.

With holy feet, and lamps bright burning,
I go to meet my Lord returning.

11.

First type, O Blessèd One, of Thee
In Abel shining bright we see:
   To heaven he lifts his eyes,
   Blood-dripping, and thus cries:
"Me, by my cruel brother slain, receive, O Lord,
   O Thou the Eternal Word."

THE REFRAIN.

With holy feet, and lamps bright burning,
I go to meet my Lord returning.

12.

Joseph, another type of Thee,
Won highest prize of purity:
  Whom Thou wouldst own Thy child:
  He scorned to be beguiled
By shameless woman; stripped, he yet her wrath defied,
  And straight to Thee he cried:

THE REFRAIN.

With holy feet, and lamps bright burning,
I go to meet my Lord returning.

13.

A lamb for sacrifice is sought:
A lamb-like victim Jephthah brought:
  For rash-made vow he cared,
  Nor virgin daughter spared:
A type, O Blessèd One, of Thy humanity,
  She poured her soul to Thee:

THE REFRAIN.

With holy feet, and lamps bright burning,
I go to meet my Lord returning.

14.

In valour Judith holds high post:
The leader of the oppressing host
    She smote by beauty's lure,
    Herself a type all pure:
He headless lay; and unto Thee the conquering maid
    Her love in song displayed:

THE REFRAIN.

With holy feet, and lamps bright burning,
I go to meet my Lord returning.

15.

The judges twain, by passion's flame
Enkindled, and all dead to shame,
    Would chaste Susannah bind
    To their unhallowed mind:
To their proposals base she gave a just reply:
    And raised her voice on high:

THE REFRAIN.

With holy feet, and lamps bright burning,
I go to meet my Lord returning.

16.

'Twere better far that I should die,
Than traitress be to marriage tie,
    And yielding to your will
    Both soul and body kill :
Base men ! God's fire of wrath eternal would me
    seize :
    Save me, O Christ, from these !

THE REFRAIN.

With holy feet, and lamps bright burning,
I go to meet my Lord returning.

17.

And he who thousands washed from sin,
Of Thy true light the bringer-in,
    For virtue's cause alone
    Is into prison thrown
By wicked king : and staining now the ground with
    gore,
    He cried to Thee the more :

THE REFRAIN.

With holy feet, and lamps bright burning,
I go to meet my Lord returning.

18.

And Thy blest Mother, spotless maid,
Was thought her vows to have betrayed,
   When travailing with Thee,
   O Lord of purity:
And found with child of transcendental heavenly birth,
   She raised her voice from earth:

THE REFRAIN.

With holy feet, and lamps bright burning,
I go to meet my Lord returning.

19.

Thy saints, all eager that they may
Behold the glories of the day
   Of Thine espousals high,
   With holy gifts draw nigh:
For Thou, O Word, hast called them, Thou the angels' King:
   White-robed to Thee they sing.

THE REFRAIN.

With holy feet, and lamps bright burning,
I go to meet my Lord returning.

20.

O holy Church, O heavenly Bride,
With hymns, attending at Thy side,
   We yet on earth below
   Thine honour thus forth-show :
All snow-white thou, all beauteous spouse of Christ above,
   All purity, all love.

THE REFRAIN.

With holy feet, and lamps bright burning,
I go to meet my Lord returning.

21.

Past are corruption, sickness, pain ;
Nor tears shall ever flow again ;
   For troubles all have fled ;
   And death himself is dead :
And sin and folly with dark dismal train are gone,
   Since grace in glory shone.

THE REFRAIN.

With holy feet, and lamps bright burning,
I go to meet my Lord returning.

22.

No longer Paradise of men
Is void; for *there* God wills again
  That man should safely dwell;
  Yea, man the same who fell
Beneath the serpent's wiles: now in the promised rest,
  Immortal, fearless, blest.

THE REFRAIN.

With holy feet, and lamps bright burning,
I go to meet my Lord returning.

23.

Thou now to heavenly places raised,
By all the virgin choir art praised,
  O Bride of Heavenly King:
  And song all new we sing:
With lighted torch in hand, with snow-white lilies
  crowned,
  Thy praise in Christ we sound.

THE REFRAIN.

With holy feet, and lamps bright burning,
I go to meet my Lord returning.

24.

Father of heaven, supreme in might,
Dwelling in pure eternal light
 With Thine own Son most dear,
 Admit—for we are here—
E'en us within the gates of life, to sing Thy love
 In Thy blest courts above.

THE REFRAIN.

With holy feet, and lamps bright burning,
I go to meet my Lord returning.

CLEMENT

OF ALEXANDRIA

(A.D. 170–220).

THIS is probably the oldest hymn in the volume, as Titus Flavius Clement, the Presbyter and illustrious head of the Catechetical School at Alexandria, flourished towards the end of the second and the beginning of the third century. I had completed my translation of this celebrated hymn, before I was aware that it had been translated by Dr. W. L. Alexander.[1]

In my translation I have followed the arrangement of the learned editors of the *Anthologia Græca*, beginning with what in other editions stands as the ninth line.

---

[1] See *Writings of Clement of Alexandria*, vol. i. pp. 341-345, *Antenicene Christian Library*.

HYMN TO CHRIST.

Clement of Alexandria.

Anapæstic Dimeter.

O Thou, the King of saints, all-conquering Word,
Son of the Highest, wisdom's Fount and Lord,
The prop that doth uphold through toil and pain,
The joy of ages through immortal reign;
Yet born of mortal flesh for life's brief span.
O Saviour Jesus, Shepherd, Husbandman;
Helm Thou to guide, and bridle to restrain,
Wing of the holy flock that heaven would gain;
Catcher of men from evil's whelming sea,
The holy fishes, saved that are to be.
Drawn from the billowy deep with sweetest lure
Of life that shall for evermore endure;
O holiest Shepherd of enlightened sheep,
Lead Thou Thy flock the upward heavenly steep.

O King of holy children, lead the way,
And pure may they both follow and obey!
Thou art, O Christ, the living heavenly Way,
The ever-flowing Word, unchanging Day,
Eternal Light, and mercy's healthful Spring;
The Perfecter of every virtuous thing; 20
Pure Life of all the happy ransomed throng
Who hymn their God through all the ages long:
The heavenly [1] milk, from holy breasts that flows,
By which the infant Church in wisdom grows,
And graces rare, as it befits the Bride,
Adorned, O Jesu Christ, for Thine own side.
Thy feeble children gather with sweet smile,
To sing with holy mouth, and free from guile,
Thyself, in songs and praises without end,
The children's leader, and the children's friend. 30

O little children, thus so gently led,
So tenderly with truth and reason fed,
And fillèd with the Holy Spirit's dew,
Our hymns and praises feeble, yet all true,

---

[1] In this disputed passage, which I have ventured to render freely, I take the γάλα to be Christ Himself, in same way as βιοτή, πηγή, &c., above, and read ἐκθλιβόμενον.

In grateful homage unto Christ the King,
Who taught us life, let us together sing :
A peaceful choir, Christ-born, and undefiled,
A people wise, sing we the strong-born child ;
Sing we with heart and voice, and never cease
To praise with one accord the God of Peace !   40

POSTSCRIPT

THE task which I had set myself to do is completed. Whatever may be the fortune of the little work, I have had much pleasure, and, I hope, some profit, in the accomplishment of it.

At intervals from parochial visiting and ministerial duty, on a walk, or reclining by the Wye side, or on the ridge of Marcle Hill, I have made, bit by bit, the translation of the first, the earlier and shorter, part of the *Anthologia Græca Carminum Christianorum*. I have had no other edition, no explanatory notes, no help or guidance—nothing but the text of the beautiful Leipsic volume, edited in 1871 by the eminent scholars, W. Christ and M. Paranikas. Under such circumstances, it can hardly be otherwise than that I have made blunders which the learned reader will detect here and there, yet I trust the errors will be few and pardonable. Owing to the difference of idiom, and the exigency of metre, some additions, some omissions, there must be. Yet I hope to be able to claim the credit of having fairly and faithfully reproduced the poetic thoughts and holy aspirations of the grand old Greek Christians whose songs and hymns I have ventured to take in hand.

There remain four short hymns of unknown authorship (ὕμνοι ἀδέσποτοι), not in verse, but measured prose. These I now render into plain English, line for line and word for word. They are, I doubt not, true specimens of the "psalms and hymns and spiritual songs"[1] of the earliest Christians, portions of the divine poetry of the Old Testament combined with the glorious facts and truths of the New. They show also the great antiquity of parts of the Church of England Liturgy and Communion Service, and may well be used now in the way they were designed of old.

[1] Eph. v. 9; Col. iii. 16.

HYMNS

OF UNKNOWN AUTHORSHIP.

I.

A MORNING HYMN.

GLORY to God in the highest, and upon earth peace,
    Good-will among men :
We praise Thee, we bless Thee, we give thanks to
    Thee,
    We worship Thee, we glorify Thee.
    For Thy great glory.
O Lord the King in heaven, God the Father Almighty,
    O Lord the only-begotten Son, Jesus Christ,
    And Holy Spirit :
O Lord God, Lamb of God, Son of the Father,
    Who takest[1] away the sins of the world, have
        mercy upon us :
    O Thou who takest away the sins of the world,
        receive our prayer :

---

[1] αἴρεις, takest away, or bearest.

O Thou who sittest at the right hand of the
Father, have mercy upon us:
For Thou only art holy, Thou only art the Lord,
Jesus Christ, to the glory of God the Father.

Amen.

Every day will I bless Thee,
And praise Thy Name for ever,[1]
And for ever and ever.
Vouchsafe, O Lord, through this day also
That we may be kept without sin.
Blessed art Thou, O Lord God of our fathers,
And praised and glorified be Thy Name
For ever and ever.[2]   Amen.

Blessed art Thou, O Lord: teach me Thy judgments.
Blessed art Thou, O Lord: teach me Thy judgments.
Blessed art Thou, O Lord: teach me Thy judgments.
O Lord, Thou hast been our refuge from generation
to generation:
I have said: O Lord, have mercy upon me,
Heal my soul, for I have sinned against Thee.

---

[1] Lit.: For the age, and for the age of the age.
[2] Lit.: For the ages.

O Lord, to Thee have I fled for refuge : teach me to
> do Thy will,
> For Thou art my God,
> For with Thee is the fountain of life.

In Thy light shall we see light :
> Extend Thy mercy to them that know Thee.

II.

AN EVENING HYMN.

PRAISE the Lord, O ye His servants,[1]
    Praise the Name of the Lord :
We praise Thee, we hymn Thee, we bless Thee
    For Thy great glory.
O Lord the King, the Father of Christ, the Lamb without blemish,
    Who taketh away the sin of the world,
To Thee belongeth praise, to Thee belongeth the hymn, to Thee belongeth glory,
    The Father, and the Son, and the Holy Spirit,
    Throughout all ages.[2] Amen.
Now lettest Thou Thy servant depart, O Lord,
    According to Thy word, in peace :
For mine eyes have seen Thy salvation,
Which Thou hast prepared before the face of all people,
A light to lighten the Gentiles, and (to be) the glory of Thy people Israel.

---

[1] παῖδες, servants, or children.   [2] Lit.: For the ages of ages.

III.

A HYMN AT LAMP-LIGHT.

PROPITIOUS Light of holy glory,
Of the Immortal Heavenly Father,
Holy, blessed,
O Jesu Christ,
Having come to the setting of the sun,
Having seen the evening light,
We hymn the Father, the Son,
And the Holy Spirit, God.
Thou art worthy at all seasons
To be hymned with thankful [1] voices,
O Son of God, who givest life ;
Wherefore the world glorifieth Thee.

[1] αἰσίαις, lit. auspicious.

IV.

A PRAYER AT DINNER-TIME.

THOU art blessed, O Lord, who nourishest me from my youth,
    Who givest food to all flesh.
Fill your hearts with joy and gladness,
That at all times having all sufficiency,
    We may abound to every good work
    In Christ Jesus our Lord:
With whom to Thee (be) glory, honour, and might,
    For ever and ever. Amen.

FINIS.

LONDON: PRINTED BY WILLIAM CLOWES AND SONS, STAMFORD STREET
AND CHARING CROSS.

July, 1876.

A CLASSIFIED CATALOGUE OF BOOKS

Selected from the Publications of

Messrs. RIVINGTON

WATERLOO PLACE, LONDON

HIGH STREET, OXFORD; TRINITY STREET, CAMBRIDGE

Contents.

	PAGE		PAGE
1. THE PRAYER BOOK AND THE CHURCH SERVICE	1	6. SERMONS	47
		7. RELIGIOUS EDUCATION	65
2. THE HOLY SCRIPTURES	7	8. ALLEGORIES AND TALES	70
3. DEVOTIONAL WORKS	17, 88	9. HISTORY AND BIOGRAPHY	73
4. PARISH WORK	32	10. POETRY AND MISCELLANEOUS	84
5. THE CHURCH AND DOCTRINE	37	11. INDEX	89

EDUCATIONAL WORKS—*see* RIVINGTON'S SCHOOL CATALOGUE.

1. The Prayer Book and the Church Service.

The Compendious Edition of the Annotated Book of Common Prayer, forming a concise Commentary on the Devotional System of the Church of England. By the Rev. JOHN HENRY BLUNT, M.A., F.S.A., Editor of the "Dictionary of Sects and Heresies," &c., &c. Crown 8vo. 10*s.* 6*d.*; in half-morocco, 16*s.*; or in morocco limp, 17*s.* 6*d.*

[D—502]   Waterloo Place, London

The Annotated Book of Common

Prayer; being an Historical, Ritual, and Theological Commentary on the Devotional System of the Church of England. Edited by the Rev. JOHN HENRY BLUNT, M.A., F.S.A., Editor of the "Dictionary of Sects and Heresies," &c., &c. Sixth Edition. Imperial 8vo. 36s.; or in half-morocco, 48s.

[This large edition contains the Latin and Greek originals, together with technical Ritual Annotations, Marginal References, &c., which are necessarily omitted for want of room in the "Compendious Edition."]

"*Whether as, historically, shewing how the Prayer Book came to be what it is, or, ritually, how it designs itself to be rendered from word into act, or, theologically, as exhibiting the relation between doctrine and worship on which it is framed, the book amasses a world of information carefully digested, and errs commonly, if at all, on the side of excess.*"—GUARDIAN.

"*The most complete and compendious Commentary on the English Prayer Book ever yet published. Almost everything that has been written by all the best liturgical and historical authorities ancient and modern (of which a formidable list is prefixed to the work) is quoted, or referred to, or compressed into the notes illustrative of the several subjects.*"—JOHN BULL.

"*The book is a mine of information and research—able to give an answer almost on anything we wish to know about our present Prayer Book, its antecedents and originals—and ought to be in the library of every intelligent Churchman. Nothing at all like it has as yet been seen.*"—CHURCH REVIEW.

Liber Precum Publicarum Ecclesiæ

Anglicanæ. A GULIELMO BRIGHT, D.D., et PETRO GOLDSMITH MEDD, A.M., Presbyteris, Collegii Universitatis in Acad. Oxon. Sociis, Latine redditus. New Edition. With Rubrics in Red. Small 8vo. 6s.

The First Book of Common Prayer of

Edward VI. and the Ordinal of 1549. Together with the Order of the Communion, 1548. Reprinted entire. Edited by the Rev. HENRY BASKERVILLE WALTON, M.A., late Fellow and Tutor of Merton College; with Introduction by the Rev. PETER GOLDSMITH MEDD, M.A., Rector of North Cerney, Gloucestershire, late Senior Fellow of University College, Oxford. Small 8vo. 6s.

Waterloo Place, London

The Prayer Book Interleaved; with

Historical Illustrations and Explanatory Notes arranged parallel to the Text. By W. M. CAMPION, D.D., and W. J. BEAMONT, M.A. With a Preface by the LORD BISHOP OF ELY. Eighth Edition. Small 8vo. 7s. 6d.

"*An excellent publication, combining a portable Prayer Book with the history of the text and explanatory notes.*"—SPECTATOR.

"*This book is of the greatest use for spreading an intelligent knowledge of the English Prayer Book, and we heartily wish it a large and continuous circulation.*"—CHURCH REVIEW.

"*The work may be commended as a very convenient manual for all who are interested to some extent in liturgical studies, but who have not time or the means for original research. It would also be most useful to examining chaplains, as a text-book for Holy Orders.*"—CHURCH TIMES.

The Book of Common Prayer, and

Administration of the Sacraments and other Rites and Ceremonies of the Church, according to the use of THE PROTESTANT EPISCOPAL CHURCH in the UNITED STATES of AMERICA, together with the Psalter, or Psalms of David. Royal 32mo. French Roan limp, 2s. 6d.

An Illuminated Edition of the Book

of Common Prayer, printed in Red and Black, on fine toned paper; with Borders and Titles designed after the manner of the 14th Century. By R. R. HOLMES, F.S.A., and engraved by O. JEWITT. Crown 8vo. 16s.; or in morocco elegant, 21s.

A Book of Litanies, Metrical and Prose.

With an Evening Service. Edited by the Compiler of "The Treasury of Devotion." And accompanying Music arranged under the Musical Editorship of W. S. HOYTE, Organist and Director of the Choir at All Saints', Margaret Street, London. Crown 4to. 7s. 6d.

Also may be had, an Edition of the Words, 32mo., 6d.; or in paper cover, 4d. Or, the Metrical Litanies separately, 32mo., 5d.; or in paper cover, 3d.

and at Oxford and Cambridge

A Key to the Knowledge and Use of
the Book of Common Prayer. By the Rev. JOHN HENRY BLUNT, M.A., F.S.A., Editor of the "Annotated Book of Common Prayer," &c. New Edition. Small 8vo. 2s. 6d.

Forming a Volume of "Keys to Christian Knowledge."

"*Impossible to praise too highly. It is the best short explanation of our offices that we know of, and would be invaluable for the use of candidates for confirmation in the higher classes.*"—JOHN BULL.

"*A very valuable and practical manual, full of information, which is admirably calculated to instruct and interest those for whom it was evidently specially intended—the laity of the Church of England. It deserves high commendation.*"—CHURCHMAN.

"*A thoroughly sound and valuable manual.*"—CHURCH TIMES.

"*To us it appears that Mr. Blunt has succeeded very well. All necessary information seems to be included, and the arrangement is excellent.*"—LITERARY CHURCHMAN.

Sacraments and Sacramental Ordinances of the Church;
being a Plain Exposition of their History, Meaning, and Effects. By the Rev. JOHN HENRY BLUNT, M.A., F.S.A., Editor of the "Annotated Book of Common Prayer," &c. Small 8vo. 4s. 6d.

A Commentary, Expository and Devotional,
on the Order of the Administration of the Lord's Supper, according to the Use of the Church of England; to which is added, an Appendix on Fasting Communion, Non-communicating Attendance, Auricular Confession, the Doctrine of Sacrifice, and the Eucharistic Sacrifice. By EDWARD MEYRICK GOULBURN, D.D., Dean of Norwich. Sixth Edition. Small 8vo. 6s.

Also a Cheap Edition, uniform with "Thoughts on Personal Religion," and "The Pursuit of Holiness." 3s. 6d.

Notitia Eucharistica; a Commentary,
Explanatory, Doctrinal, and Historical, on the Order for the Administration of the Lord's Supper, or Holy Communion, according to the use of the Church of England. With an Appendix on the Office for the Communion of the Sick. By the Rev. W. E. SCUDAMORE, M.A., Rector of Ditchingham, and formerly Fellow of St. John's College, Cambridge. Second Edition, revised and enlarged. 8vo. 32s.

The Athanasian Creed: an Examination

of Recent Theories respecting its Date and Origin. With a Postscript referring to Professor Swainson's Account of its Growth and Reception, which is contained in his Work entitled "The Nicene and Apostles' Creeds, their Literary History." By G. D. W. OMMANNEY, M.A., Vicar of Draycot, Somerset. Crown 8vo. 8s. 6d.

The Athanasian Origin of the Athan-

asian Creed. By J. S. BREWER, M.A., Preacher at the Rolls, and Honorary Fellow of Queen's College, Oxford. Crown 8vo. 3s. 6d.

The "Damnatory Clauses" of the

Athanasian Creed rationally explained in a Letter to the Right Hon. W. E. GLADSTONE, M.P. By the Rev. MALCOLM MACCOLL, M.A., Rector of St. George, Botolph Lane. Crown 8vo. 6s.

Comment upon the Collects appointed

to be used in the Church of England on Sundays and Holy Days throughout the Year. By JOHN JAMES, D.D., sometime Canon of Peterborough. Fifteenth Edition. 12mo. 3s. 6d.

A Commentary, Practical and Exegeti-

cal, on the Lord's Prayer. By the Rev. W. DENTON, M.A. Small 8vo. 5s.

The Psalter, or Psalms of David, pointed

as they are to be sung or said in Churches. Printed in red and black. Small 8vo. 2s. 6d.

---

and at Oxford and Cambridge

The New Mitre Hymnal, containing New

Music by Sir JOHN GOSS, Sir GEORGE ELVEY, Dr. STAINER, HENRY GADSBY, Esq., J. BAPTISTE CALKIN, Esq., BERTHOLD TOURS, Esq., JAMES LANGRAN, Esq., and other eminent Composers; together with Scandinavian Tunes now first introduced into this Country. Royal 8vo. 5s.

An Edition of the Words without the Music may also be had. Imperial 32mo., cloth limp, 1s.; or in cloth boards, extra gilt, 1s. 6d.

[A large reduction to purchasers of quantities.]

Psalms and Hymns adapted to the

Services of the Church of England; with a Supplement of additional Hymns, and Indices. By the Rev. W. J. HALL, M.A. 8vo., 5s. 6d.; 18mo., 3s.; 24mo., 1s. 6d.; cloth limp, 1s. 3d.; 32mo., 1s.; cloth limp, 8d.

Selection of Psalms and Hymns; with

Accompanying Tunes selected and arranged by JOHN FOSTER, of Her Majesty's Chapels Royal. By the Rev. W. J. HALL, M.A. Crown 8vo. 2s. 6d. The Tunes only, 1s. Also an Edition of the Tunes for the Organ. 7s. 6d.

Waterloo Place, London

2. The Holy Scriptures.

The Greek Testament. With a Critically
Revised Text; a Digest of Various Readings; Marginal References to Verbal and Idiomatic Usage; Prolegomena; and a Critical and Exegetical Commentary. For the use of Theological Students and Ministers. By HENRY ALFORD, D.D., late Dean of Canterbury. New Edition. 4 Volumes. 8vo. 120s.

The Volumes are sold separately, as follows :—

Vol. I.—The Four Gospels. 28s.
Vol. II.—Acts to 2 Corinthians. 24s.
Vol. III.—Galatians to Philemon. 18s.
Vol. IV.—Hebrews to Revelation. 32s.

The New Testament for English
Readers : containing the Authorized Version, with a revised English Text; Marginal References; and a Critical and Explanatory Commentary. By HENRY ALFORD, D.D., late Dean of Canterbury. New Edition. 2 Volumes, or 4 Parts. 8vo. 54s. 6d.

The Volumes are sold separately, as follows :—

Vol. 1, Part I.—The Three first Gospels. 12s.
Vol. 1, Part II.—St. John and the Acts. 10s. 6d.
Vol. 2, Part I.—The Epistles of St. Paul. 16s.
Vol. 2, Part II.—Hebrews to Revelation. 16s.

---

and at Oxford and Cambridge

The Holy Bible; with Notes and Introductions.

By CHR. WORDSWORTH, D.D., Bishop of Lincoln. New Edition. 6 Vols. Imperial 8vo. 120s.

> The Volumes are sold separately, as follows:—
>
> Vol. I.—The Pentateuch. 25s.
> Vol. II.—Joshua to Samuel. 15s.
> Vol. III.—Kings to Esther. 15s.
> Vol. IV.—Job to Song of Solomon. 25s.
> Vol. V.—Isaiah to Ezekiel. 25s.
> Vol. VI.—Daniel, Minor Prophets, and Index. 15s.

The New Testament of our Lord and

Saviour JESUS CHRIST, in the original Greek; with Notes, Introductions, and Indices. By CHR. WORDSWORTH, D.D., Bishop of Lincoln. New Edition. 2 Vols. Imperial 8vo. 60s.

> The Volumes are sold separately, as follows:—
>
> Vol. I.—Gospels and Acts. 23s.
> Vol. II.—Epistles, Apocalypse, and Index. 37s.

Notes on the Greek Testament. The

Gospel according to S. Luke. By the Rev. ARTHUR CARR, M.A., Assistant-Master at Wellington College, late Fellow of Oriel College, Oxford. Crown 8vo. 6s.

"It is a most useful and scholarly work, well adapted to the higher classes of public schools and the students at our colleges."—STANDARD.

"The most useful and scholarly commentary, in a short compass, on the Gospel of S. Luke, in Greek, that has hitherto appeared."—HOUR.

"The notes are brief, scholarly, and based on the best authorities.... The introduction will be found to be of especial value to the young student, informing him, as it does, of the Greek manuscripts which form the basis of the Greek text, and giving a most thorough and comprehensive account of S. Luke's life and the style of his writing."—SCHOOL BOARD CHRONICLE.

"Grammatical peculiarities are brought into the foreground, and contrasted with classical usages; questions of various reading are carefully noted; historical and archæological information is supplied plentifully when needful to illustrate a passage; the drift of a narrative or discourse and the sequence of the thoughts is traced out and carefully analysed; in short, the Gospel is treated as we treat a classical author, and the student is here supplied with an apparatus criticus superior in kind and completeness to any we have ever seen afforded to him for the purpose elsewhere. A very clever and taking book."—LITERARY CHURCHMAN.

"Admirably adapted for the use of those who begin the study of the New Testament in the original after having acquired a fair acquaintance with classical Greek."—SCOTSMAN.

The Psalms. Translated from the Hebrew.
With Notes, chiefly Exegetical. By WILLIAM KAY, D.D., Rector of Great Leghs, late Principal of Bishop's College, Calcutta. Second Edition. 8vo. 12s. 6d.

"*Like a sound Churchman, he reverences Scripture, upholding its authority against sceptics; and he does not denounce such as differ from him in opinion with a dogmatism unhappily too common at the present day. Hence, readers will be disposed to consider his conclusions worthy of attention; or perhaps to adopt them without inquiry. It is superfluous to say that the translation is better and more accurate on the whole than our received one, or that it often reproduces the sense of the original happily.*"—ATHENÆUM.

"*Dr. Kay has profound reverence for Divine truth, and exhibits considerable reading, with the power to make use of it.*"—BRITISH QUARTERLY REVIEW.

"*The execution of the work is careful and scholarly.*"—UNION REVIEW.

"*To mention the name of Dr. Kay is enough to secure respectful attention to his new translation of the Psalms. It is enriched with exegetical notes containing a wealth of sound learning, closely occasionally, perhaps too closely condensed. Good care is taken of the student not learned in Hebrew; we hope the Doctor's example will prevent any abuse of this consideration, and stimulate those who profit by it to follow him into the very text of the ancient Revelation.*"—JOHN BULL.

Ecclesiastes: the Authorized Version, with
a running Commentary and Paraphrase. By the Rev. THOS. PELHAM DALE, M.A., Rector of St. Vedast with St. Michael City of London, and late Fellow of Sidney Sussex College, Cambridge. 8vo. 7s. 6d.

Daniel the Prophet: Nine Lectures
delivered in the Divinity School of the University of Oxford. With copious Notes. By the Rev. E. B. PUSEY, D.D., Regius Professor of Hebrew, Canon of Christ Church, Oxford. Third Edition. 8vo. 10s. 6d.

Commentary on the Minor Prophets;
with Introductions to the several Books. By the Rev. E. B. PUSEY, D.D., Regius Professor of Hebrew, Canon of Christ Church, Oxford. 4to.

Parts I., II., III., IV., V., 5s. each.

A Companion to the Old Testament;

being a Plain Commentary on Scripture History, down to the Birth of our Lord. Small 8vo. 3s. 6d.

Also in 2 Parts:

Part I.—The Creation of the World to the Reign of Saul.
Part II.—The Reign of Saul to the Birth of Our Lord.

Small 8vo. 2s. each.

[Especially adapted for use in Training Colleges and Schools.]

"*A very compact summary of the Old Testament narrative, put together so as to explain the connection and bearing of its contents, and written in a very good tone; with a final chapter on the history of the Jews between the Old and New Testaments. It will be found very useful for its purpose. It does not confine itself to merely chronological difficulties, but comments briefly upon the religious bearing of the text also.*"—GUARDIAN.

"*A most admirable Companion to the Old Testament, being far the most concise yet complete commentary on Old Testament history with which we have met. Here are combined orthodoxy and learning, an intelligent and at the same time interesting summary of the leading facts of the sacred story. It should be a text-book in every school, and its value is immensely enhanced by the copious and complete index.*"—JOHN BULL.

"*This will be found a very valuable aid to the right understanding of the Bible. It throws the whole Scripture narrative into one from the creation downwards, the author thus condensing Prideaux, Shuckford, and Russell, and in the most reverential manner bringing to his aid the writings of all modern annotators and chronologists. The book is one that should have a wide circulation amongst teachers and students of all denominations.*"—BOOKSELLER.

"*The handbook before us is so full and satisfactory, considering its compass, and sets forth the history of the old covenant with such conscientious minuteness, that it cannot fail to prove a godsend to candidates for examination in the Rudimenta Religionis as well as in the corresponding school at Cambridge. . . . Enough has been said to express our value of this useful work, which cannot fail to win its way into our schools, colleges, and universities.*"—ENGLISH CHURCHMAN.

Commentary on the Book of Isaiah,

Critical, Historical, and Prophetical: including a Revised English Translation. With Introduction and Appendices on the Nature of Scripture Prophecy, the Life and Times of Isaiah, the Genuineness of the later Prophecies, the Structure and History of the whole Book, the Assyrian History in Isaiah's days, and various difficult passages. By the Rev. T. R. BIRKS, M.A., Vicar of Holy Trinity, Cambridge. 8vo. 12s.

Waterloo Place, London

A Key to the Narrative of the Four

Gospels. By the Rev. JOHN PILKINGTON NORRIS, B.D., Canon of Bristol, and Examining Chaplain to the Bishop of Manchester. New Edition. Small 8vo. 2s. 6d.

Forming a Volume of "Keys to Christian Knowledge."

"*This is very much the best book of its kind we have seen. The only fault is its shortness, which prevents its going into the details which would support and illustrate its statements, and which, in the process of illustrating them, would fix them upon the minds and memories of its readers. It is, however, a great improvement upon any book of its kind we know. It bears all the marks of being the condensed work of a real scholar, and of a divine too. The bulk of the book is taken up with a 'Life of Christ,' compiled from the Four Gospels, so as to exhibit its steps and stages and salient points. The rest of the book consists of independent chapters on special points.*"—LITERARY CHURCHMAN.

"*This book is no ordinary compendium, no mere 'cram-book;' still less is it an ordinary reading-book for schools; but the schoolmaster, the Sunday-school teacher, and the seeker after a comprehensive knowledge of Divine truth will find it worthy of its name. Canon Norris writes simply, reverently, without great display of learning, giving the result of much careful study in a short compass, and adorning the subject by the tenderness and honesty with which he treats it. We hope that this little book will have a very wide circulation, and that it will be studied; and we can promise that those who take it up will not readily put it down again.*"—RECORD.

"*This is a golden little volume. . . . Its design is exceedingly modest. Canon Norris writes primarily to help 'younger students' in studying the Gospels. But this unpretending volume is one which all students may study with advantage. It is an admirable manual for those who take Bible Classes through the Gospels. Closely sifted in style, so that all is clear and weighty; full of unostentatious learning, and pregnant with suggestion; deeply reverent in spirit and altogether Evangelical in spirit; Canon Norris's book supplies a real want, and ought to be welcomed by all earnest and devout students of the Holy Gospels.*"—LONDON QUARTERLY REVIEW.

A Key to the Narrative of the Acts of

the Apostles. By the Rev. JOHN PILKINGTON NORRIS, B.D., Canon of Bristol, and Examining Chaplain to the Bishop of Manchester. New Edition. Small 8vo. 2s. 6d.

Forming a Volume of "Keys to Christian Knowledge."

"*The book is one which we can heartily recommend.*"—SPECTATOR.

"*Few books have ever given us more unmixed pleasure than this.*"—LITERARY CHURCHMAN.

"*This is a sequel to Canon Norris's 'Key to the Gospels,' which was published two years ago, and which has become a general favourite with those who wish to grasp the leading features of the life and work of Christ. The sketch of the Acts of the Apostles is done in the same style; there is the same reverent spirit and quiet enthusiasm running through it, and the same instinct for seizing the leading points in the narrative.*"—RECORD.

and at Oxford and Cambridge

A Devotional Commentary on the

Gospel Narrative. By the Rev. ISAAC WILLIAMS, B.D., formerly Fellow of Trinity College, Oxford. New Edition. 8 Vols. Crown 8vo. 5s. each. Sold separately.

THOUGHTS ON THE STUDY OF THE HOLY GOSPELS.

Characteristic Differences in the Four Gospels—Our Lord's Manifestations of Himself—The Rule of Scriptural Interpretation furnished by our Lord—Analogies of the Gospel—Mention of Angels in the Gospels—Places of our Lord's Abode and Ministry—Our Lord's mode of dealing with His Apostles—Conclusion.

A HARMONY OF THE FOUR EVANGELISTS.

Our Lord's Nativity—Our Lord's Ministry (second year)—Our Lord's Ministry (third year)—The Holy Week—Our Lord's Passion—Our Lord's Resurrection.

OUR LORD'S NATIVITY.

The Birth at Bethlehem—The Baptism in Jordan—The First Passover.

OUR LORD'S MINISTRY (Second Year).

The Second Passover—Christ with the Twelve—The Twelve sent forth.

OUR LORD'S MINISTRY (Third Year).

Teaching in Galilee—Teaching at Jerusalem—Last Journey from Galilee to Jerusalem.

THE HOLY WEEK.

The Approach to Jerusalem—The Teaching in the Temple—The Discourse on the Mount of Olives—The Last Supper.

OUR LORD'S PASSION.

The Hour of Darkness—The Agony—The Apprehension—The Condemnation—The Day of Sorrows—The Hall of Judgment—The Crucifixion—The Sepulture.

OUR LORD'S RESURRECTION.

The Day of Days—The Grave Visited—Christ appearing—The going to Emmaus—The Forty Days—The Apostles assembled—The Lake in Galilee—The Mountain in Galilee—The Return from Galilee.

"*There is not a better companion to be found for the season than the beautiful 'Devotional Commentary on the Gospel Narrative,' by the Rev. Isaac Williams. A rich mine for devotional and theological study.*"—GUARDIAN.

"*So infinite are the depths and so innumerable the beauties of Scripture, and more particularly of the Gospels, that there is some difficulty in describing the manifold excellences of Williams' exquisite Commentary. Deriving its profound appreciation of Scripture from the writings of the early Fathers, it is only what every student knows must be true to say, that it extracts a whole wealth of meaning from each sentence, each apparently faint allusion, each word in the text.*"—CHURCH REVIEW.

"*Stands absolutely alone in our English literature; there is, we should say, no chance of its being superseded by any better book of its kind; and its merits are of the very highest order.*"—LITERARY CHURCHMAN.

Waterloo Place, London

The Holy Scriptures

WILLIAMS' DEVOTIONAL COMMENTARY—*Continued.*

"*This is, in the truest sense of the word, a 'Devotional Commentary' on the Gospel narrative, opening out everywhere, as it does, the spiritual beauties and blessedness of the Divine message; but it is something more than this, it meets difficulties almost by anticipation, and throws the light of learning over some of the very darkest passages in the New Testament.*"—ROCK.

"*It would be difficult to select a more useful present, at a small cost, than this series would be to a young man on his first entering into Holy Orders, and many, no doubt, will avail themselves of the republication of these useful volumes for this purpose. There is an abundance of sermon material to be drawn from any one of them.*"—CHURCH TIMES.

Female Characters of Holy Scripture.

A Series of Sermons. By the Rev. ISAAC WILLIAMS, B.D., formerly Fellow of Trinity College, Oxford. New Edition. Crown 8vo. 5*s*.

CONTENTS.

Eve—Sarah—Lot's Wife—Rebekah—Leah and Rachel—Miriam—Rahab—Deborah—Ruth—Hannah—The Witch of Endor—Bathsheba—Rizpah—The Queen of Sheba—The Widow of Zarephath—Jezebel—The Shunammite—Esther—Elizabeth—Anna—The Woman of Samaria—Joanna—The Woman with the Issue of Blood—The Woman of Canaan—Martha—Mary—Salome—The Wife of Pilate—Dorcas—The Blessed Virgin.

The Characters of the Old Testament.

A Series of Sermons. By the Rev. ISAAC WILLIAMS, B.D., formerly Fellow of Trinity College, Oxford. New Edition. Crown 8vo. 5*s*.

CONTENTS.

Adam—Abel and Cain—Noah—Abraham—Lot—Jacob and Esau—Joseph—Moses—Aaron—Pharaoh—Korah, Dathan, and Abiram—Balaam—Joshua—Samson—Samuel—Saul—David—Solomon—Elijah—Ahab—Elisha—Hezekiah—Josiah—Jeremiah—Ezekiel—Daniel—Joel—Job—Isaiah—The Antichrist.

"*This is one of the few volumes of published sermons that we have been able to read with real pleasure. They are written with a chastened elegance of language, and pervaded by a spirit of earnest and simple piety. Mr. Williams is evidently what would be called a very High Churchman. Occasionally his peculiar Church views are apparent; but bating a few passages here and there, these sermons will be read with profit by all 'who profess and call themselves Christians.'*"—CONTEMPORARY REVIEW.

"*A more masterly analysis of Scriptural characters we never read, nor any which is more calculated to impress the mind of the reader with feelings of love for what is good, and abhorrence for what is evil.*"—ROCK.

The Apocalypse. With Notes and Reflections.

By the Rev. ISAAC WILLIAMS, B.D., formerly Fellow of Trinity College, Oxford. New Edition. Crown 8vo. 5*s*.

and at Oxford and Cambridge

Beginning of the Book of Genesis,
with Notes and Reflections. By the Rev. ISAAC WILLIAMS, B.D., formerly Fellow of Trinity College, Oxford. Small 8vo. 7s. 6d.

Ecclesiastes for English Readers. The
Book called by the Jews Koheleth. Newly translated, with Introduction, Analysis, and Notes. By the Rev. W. H. B. PROBY, M.A., formerly Tyrwhitt Hebrew Scholar in the University of Cambridge. 8vo. 4s. 6d.

The Ten Canticles of the Old Testament
Canon, namely, the Songs of Moses (First and Second), Deborah, Hannah, Isaiah (First, Second, and Third), Hezekiah, Jonah, and Habakkuk. Newly translated, with Notes and Remarks on their Drift and Use. By the Rev. W. H. B. PROBY, M.A., formerly Tyrwhitt Hebrew Scholar in the University of Cambridge. 8vo. 5s.

Genesis. With Notes. By the Rev. G. V.
GARLAND, M.A., late Vicar of Aslacton, Norfolk. [The Hebrew Text, with Literal Translation.] Parts I. to XIII. 8vo. In paper cover, 6d. each.

Devotional Commentary on the Gospel
according to St. Matthew. Translated from the French of QUESNEL. Crown 8vo. 7s. 6d.

The Acts of the Deacons; being a
Commentary, Critical and Practical, upon the Notices of St. Stephen and St. Philip the Evangelist, contained in the Acts of the Apostles. By EDWARD MEYRICK GOULBURN, D.D., Dean of Norwich. Second Edition. Small 8vo. 6s.

Waterloo Place, London

The Mystery of Christ: being an Examination of the Doctrine contained in the First Three Chapters of the Epistle of Paul the Apostle to the Ephesians. By GEORGE STAUNTON BARROW, M.A., Rector of Knight's Enham, Hants. Crown 8vo.

A Key to the Knowledge and Use of the Holy Bible. By the Rev. JOHN HENRY BLUNT, M.A., F.S.A., Editor of the "Dictionary of Theology," &c. &c. New Edition. Small 8vo. 2s. 6d.

Forming a Volume of "Keys to Christian Knowledge."

"*Another of Mr. Blunt's useful and workmanlike compilations, which will be most acceptable as a household book, or in schools and colleges. It is a capital book too for schoolmasters and pupil teachers. Its subject is arranged under the heads of—I. The Literary History of the Bible. II. Old Testament Writers and Writings. III. New Testament ditto. IV. Revelation and Inspiration. V. Objects of the Bible. VI. Interpretation of ditto. VII. The Bible a guide to Faith. VIII. The Apocrypha. IX. The Apocryphal Books associated with the New Testament. Lastly, there is a serviceable appendix of peculiar Bible words and their meanings.*"—LITERARY CHURCHMAN.

"*We have much pleasure in recommending a capital handbook by the learned Editor of 'The Annotated Book of Common Prayer.'*"—CHURCH TIMES.

"*Merits commendation, for the lucid and orderly arrangement in which it presents a considerable amount of valuable and interesting matter.*"—RECORD.

The Inspiration of Holy Scripture, its Nature and Proof. Eight Discourses preached before the University of Dublin. By WILLIAM LEE, D.D., Archdeacon of Dublin. Fourth Edition. 8vo. 15s.

On the Inspiration of the Bible. Five Lectures delivered at Westminster Abbey. By CHR. WORDSWORTH, D.D., Bishop of Lincoln. Eighth Edition. Small 8vo. 1s. 6d., or in paper cover, 1s.

Syntax and Synonyms of the Greek Testament. By the Rev. WILLIAM WEBSTER, M.A., late Fellow of Queen's College, Cambridge. 8vo. 9s.

and at Oxford and Cambridge

Bible Readings for Family Prayer.
By the Rev. W. H. RIDLEY, M.A., Rector of Hambleden. Crown 8vo.
    Old Testament—Genesis and Exodus. 2s.
    The Four Gospels, 3s. 6d.
        St. Matthew and St. Mark. 2s.
        St. Luke and St. John. 2s.
    The Acts of the Apostles, 2s.

A Complete Concordance to the Old
and the New Testament; or, a Dictionary, and Alphabetical Index to the Bible, in two Parts. To which is added, a Concordance to the Apocrypha. By ALEXANDER CRUDEN, M.A. With a Life of the Author, by ALEXANDER CHALMERS, F.S.A., and a Portrait. Fourteenth Edition. Demy 4to. 21s.

3. Devotional Works.

Library of Spiritual Works for English Catholics.

Elegantly printed with red borders, on extra superfine toned paper. Small 8vo. 5*s.* each.

- OF THE IMITATION OF CHRIST. In 4 Books. By THOMAS À KEMPIS. A New Translation.
- THE CHRISTIAN YEAR: Thoughts in Verse for the Sundays and Holydays throughout the Year.
- THE SPIRITUAL COMBAT; together with the Supplement and the Path of Paradise. By LAURENCE SCUPOLI. A New Translation.
- THE DEVOUT LIFE. By SAINT FRANCIS OF SALES, Bishop and Prince of Geneva. A New Translation.

The Volumes can also be had in the following extra bindings:—

	s.	d.
Morocco, stiff or limp	9	0
Morocco, thick bevelled sides, Old Style	12	0
Morocco, limp, with flap edges	11	6
Morocco, best, stiff or limp	16	0
Morocco, best, thick bevelled sides, Old Style	19	6
Russia, limp	11	6
Russia, limp, with flap edges	13	6

Most of the volumes in the above styles may be had illustrated with a beautiful selection of Photographs from Fra Angelico, 4*s.* 6*d.* extra.

Cheap Editions, 32mo, *cloth limp,* 6*d.* *each, or cloth extra, red edges,* 1*s.* *each.*

Of the Imitation of Christ.	The Hidden Life of the Soul.
The Spiritual Combat.	Spiritual Letters of Saint Francis of Sales.
The Christian Year.	

[Other Volumes are in preparation.]

and at Oxford and Cambridge

The Child Samuel. A Practical and Devotional Commentary on the Birth and Childhood of the Prophet Samuel, as recorded in 1 Sam. i., ii. 1-27, iii. Designed as a Help to Meditation on the Holy Scriptures for Children and Young Persons. By EDWARD MEYRICK GOULBURN, D.D., Dean of Norwich. Small 8vo. 5s.

The Gospel of the Childhood: a Practical and Devotional Commentary on the Single Incident of our Blessed Lord's Childhood (St. Luke ii. 41 to the end); designed as a Help to Meditation on the Holy Scriptures, for Children and Young Persons. By EDWARD MEYRICK GOULBURN, D.D., Dean of Norwich. Second Edition. Square 16mo. 5s.

Thoughts on Personal Religion; being a Treatise on the Christian Life in its Two Chief Elements, Devotion and Practice. By EDWARD MEYRICK GOULBURN, D.D., Dean of Norwich. New Edition. Small 8vo. 6s. 6d. Also a Cheap Edition, 3s. 6d. Presentation Edition, elegantly printed on Toned Paper. Two vols. Small 8vo. 10s. 6d.

The Pursuit of Holiness: a Sequel to "Thoughts on Personal Religion," intended to carry the Reader somewhat farther onward in the Spiritual Life. By EDWARD MEYRICK GOULBURN, D.D. Fourth Edition. Small 8vo. 5s. Also a Cheap Edition, 3s. 6d.

An Introduction to the Devotional Study of the Holy Scriptures. By EDWARD MEYRICK GOULBURN, D.D. Ninth Edition. Small 8vo. 3s. 6d.

Short Devotional Forms, for Morn-ing, Night, and Midnight, and for the Third, Sixth, Ninth Hours and Eventide of each Day of the Week. Arranged to meet the Exigencies of a Busy Life. By EDWARD MEYRICK GOULBURN, D.D. Fourth Edition. 32mo. 1s. 6d.

Devotional Works

The Star of Childhood: a First Book of Prayers and Instruction for Children. Compiled by a Priest. Edited by the Rev. T. T. CARTER, M.A., Rector of Clewer, Berks. With Illustrations reduced from Engravings by FRA ANGELICO. Second Edition. Royal 16mo. 2s. 6d.

The Way of Life: a Book of Prayers and Instruction for the Young at School, with a Preparation for Confirmation. Compiled by a Priest. Edited by the Rev. T. T. CARTER, M.A. Imperial 32mo. 1s. 6d.

The Path of Holiness: a First Book of Prayers, with the Service of the Holy Communion, for the Young. Compiled by a Priest. Edited by the Rev. T. T. CARTER, M.A. With Illustrations. Crown 16mo. 1s. 6d.; cloth limp, 1s.

The Treasury of Devotion: a Manual of Prayers for General and Daily Use. Compiled by a Priest. Edited by the Rev. T. T. CARTER, M.A. New Edition, in Large Type. Crown 8vo. 5s.; in morocco limp, 10s. 6d.

The Smaller Edition, Imperial 32mo. 2s. 6d.; limp cloth, 2s., or bound with the Book of Common Prayer, 3s. 6d.

The Guide to Heaven: a Book of Prayers for every Want. (For the Working Classes.) Compiled by a Priest. Edited by the Rev. T. T. CARTER, M.A. New Edition. Imperial 32mo. 1s. 6d.; cloth limp, 1s.

An Edition in Large Type. Crown 8vo. 1s. 6d.; cloth limp, 1s.

Meditations on the Life and Mysteries of Our Lord and Saviour Jesus Christ. From the French. By the Compiler of "The Treasury of Devotion." Edited by the Rev. T. T. CARTER, M.A. Crown 8vo.

    Vol. I.—The Hidden Life of Our Lord. 3s. 6d.
    Vol. II.—The Public Life of Our Lord. 2 Parts. 5s. each.
    Vol. III.—The Suffering Life and the Glorified Life of Our Lord. 3s. 6d.

and at Oxford and Cambridge

Prayers and Meditations for the Holy

Communion. By JOSEPHINE FLETCHER. With a Preface by C. J. ELLICOTT, D.D., Lord Bishop of Gloucester and Bristol. With rubrics and borders in red. Royal 32mo. 2s. 6d.

An Edition without the red rubrics. 32mo. 1s.

"*Devout beauty is the special character of this new manual, and it ought to be a favourite. Rarely has it happened to us to meet with so remarkable a combination of thorough practicalness with that almost poetic warmth which is the highest flower of genuine devotion.*"—LITERARY CHURCHMAN.

The Bishop recommends it to the newly confirmed, to the tender-hearted and the devout, as having been compiled by a youthful person, and as being marked by a peculiar ' freshness.' Having looked through the volume, we have pleasure in seconding the recommendations of the good Bishop. We know of no more suitable manual for the newly confirmed, and nothing more likely to engage the sympathies of youthful hearts. There is a union of the deepest spirit of devotion, a rich expression of experimental life, with a due recognition of the objects of faith, such as is not always to be found, but which characterises this manual in an eminent degree."—CHURCH REVIEW.

"*Among the supply of Eucharistic Manuals, one deserves special attention and commendation. 'Prayers and Meditations' merits the Bishop of Gloucester's epithets of ' warm, devout, and fresh.' And it is thoroughly English Church besides.*"—GUARDIAN.

"*We are by no means surprised that Bishop Ellicott should have been so much struck with this little work, on accidentally seeing it in manuscript, as to urge its publication, and to preface it with his commendation. The devotion which it breathes is truly fervent, and the language attractive, and as proceeding from a young person the work is altogether not a little striking.*"—RECORD.

Words to Take with Us. A Manual of

Daily and Occasional Prayers, for Private and Common Use. With Plain Instructions and Counsels on Prayer. By W. E. SCUDAMORE, M.A., Rector of Ditchingham, and formerly Fellow of S. John's College, Cambridge. New Edition, revised. Small 8vo. 2s. 6d.

"*One of the best manuals of daily and occasional prayer we have seen. At once orthodox and practical, sufficiently personal, and yet not perplexingly minute in its details, it is calculated to be of inestimable value in many a household.*"—JOHN BULL.

"*We are again pleased to see an old friend on the editorial table, in a third edition of Mr. Scudamore's well-known Manual of Prayers. The special proper collects for each day of the week, as well as those for the several seasons of the Christian year, have been most judiciously selected. The compiler moreover, while recognizing the full benefits to be derived from the Book of Common Prayer, has not feared to draw largely from the equally invaluable writings of ancient Catholicity.*"—CHURCH REVIEW.

Waterloo Place, London

Devotional Works

The Hour of Prayer; being a Manual of Devotion for the Use of Families and Schools. With a Preface by the Rev. W. E. SCUDAMORE, M.A., Rector of Ditchingham, and formerly Fellow of S. John's College, Cambridge. Crown 8vo. 3s. 6d.

Family Prayers. Compiled from various Sources (chiefly from Bishop Hamilton's Manual), and arranged on the Liturgical Principle. By EDWARD MEYRICK GOULBURN, D.D., Dean of Norwich. New Edition. Large type. Crown 8vo. 3s. 6d. Cheap Edition. 16mo. 1s.

Manual of Family Devotions, arranged from the Book of Common Prayer. By the Hon. AUGUSTUS DUNCOMBE, D.D., Dean of York. Printed in red and black. Small 8vo. 3s. 6d.

Household Prayer, from Ancient and Authorized Sources: with Morning and Evening Readings for a Month. By the Rev. P. G. MEDD, M.A., Rector of North Cerney, Gloucestershire, and Examining Chaplain to the Bishop of Rochester. Small 8vo. 4s. 6d.

A Book of Family Prayer. Compiled by WALTER FARQUHAR HOOK, D.D., F.R.S., late Dean of Chichester. Eighth Edition, with rubrics in red. 18mo. 2s.

Daily Devotions; or, Short Morning and Evening Services for the use of a Churchman's Household. By CHARLES C. CLERKE, D.D., Archdeacon of Oxford. 18mo. 1s.

Aids to Prayer; or, Thoughts on the Practice of Devotion. With Forms of Prayer for Private Use. By DANIEL MOORE, M.A., Chaplain in Ordinary to the Queen, and Vicar of Holy Trinity, Paddington. Second Edition. Square 32mo. 2s. 6d.

and at 𝔒xford and 𝔒ambridge

Self-Renunciation. From the French.

With an Introduction by the Rev. T. T. CARTER, M.A., Rector of Clewer, Berks. Crown 8vo. 6s.

"*It is excessively difficult to review or criticise, in detail, a book of this kind, and yet its abounding merits, its practicalness, its searching good sense and thoroughness, and its frequent beauty, too, make us wish to do something more than announce its publication. . . . . The style is eminently clear, free from redundance and prolixity.*"—LITERARY CHURCHMAN.

"*Few save Religious and those brought into immediate contact with them are, in all probability, acquainted with the French treatise of Guilloré, a portion of which is now, for the first time we believe, done into English. . . . Hence the suitableness of such a book as this for those who, in the midst of their families, are endeavouring to advance in the spiritual life. Hundreds of devout souls living in the world have been encouraged and helped by such books as Dr. Neale's 'Sermons preached in a Religious House.' For such the present work will be found appropriate, while for Religious themselves it will be invaluable.*"—CHURCH TIMES.

Spiritual Guidance. With an Introduction by the Rev. T. T. CARTER, M.A., Rector of Clewer, Berks. Crown 8vo. 6s.

EXTRACT FROM PREFACE.

["The special object of the volume is to supply practical advice in matters of conscience, such as may be generally applicable. While it offers, as it is hoped, much valuable help to Directors, it is full of suggestions, which may be useful to any one in private. It thus fulfils a double purpose, which is not, as far as I am aware, otherwise provided for, at least, not in so full and direct a manner."]

"*As a work intended for general use, it will be found to contain much valuable help, and may be profitably studied by any one who is desiring to make progress in spiritual life. Much of the contents of this little book will be found more or less applicable to all persons amid the ordinary difficulties and trials of life, and a help to the training of the mind in habits of self-discipline.*"—CHURCH TIMES.

Vita et Doctrina Jesu Christi; or,

Meditations on the Life of our Lord. By AVANCINI. In the Original Latin. Adapted to the use of the Church of England by a CLERGYMAN. Imperial 32mo. 2s. 6d.

The Virgin's Lamp: Prayers and Devout

Exercises for English Sisters. By the Rev. J. M. NEALE, D.D., late Warden of Sackville College, East Grinsted. Small 8vo. 3s. 6d.

Waterloo Place, London

Voices of Comfort. Edited by the Rev.
THOMAS VINCENT FOSBERY, M.A., sometime Vicar of St. Giles's, Reading. Second Edition. Small 8vo. 7s. 6d.

[This Volume, of prose and poetry, original and selected, aims at revealing the fountains of hope and joy which underlie the griefs and sorrows of life.
It is so divided as to afford readings for a month. The key-note of each day is given by the title prefixed to it, such as : 'The Power of the Cross of Christ, Day 6. Conflicts of the Soul, Day 17. The Communion of Saints, Day 20. The Comforter, Day 22. The Light of Hope, Day 25. The Coming of Christ, Day 28.' Each day begins with passages of Holy Scripture. These are followed by articles in prose, which are succeeded by one or more short prayers. After these are Poems or passages of poetry, and then very brief extracts in prose or verse close the section. The book is meant to meet, not merely cases of bereavement or physical suffering, but 'to minister specially to the hidden troubles of the heart, as they are silently weaving their dark threads into the web of the seemingly brightest life.']

Hymns and Poems for the Sick and
Suffering. In connexion with the Service for the Visitation of the Sick. Selected from various Authors. Edited by the Rev. THOMAS VINCENT FOSBERY, M.A., sometime Vicar of St. Giles's, Reading. New Edition. Small 8vo. 3s. 6d.

[This Volume contains 233 separate pieces; of which about 90 are by writers who lived prior to the eighteenth century; the rest are modern, and some of these original. Amongst the names of the writers (between 70 and 80 in number) occur those of Sir J. Beaumont ; Sir T. Brown ; F. Davison ; Elizabeth of Bohemia ; P. Fletcher ; G. Herbert ; Dean Hickes ; Bishop Ken ; Norris ; Quarles ; Sandys ; Bishop J. Taylor ; Henry Vaughan ; and Sir H. Wotton. And of modern writers :—Mrs. Barrett Browning ; Bishop Wilberforce ; S. T. Coleridge ; Sir R. Grant ; Miss E. Taylor ; W. Wordsworth ; Archbishop Trench ; Rev. Messrs. Chandler, Keble, Lyte, Monsell, and Moultrie.]

The Christian Year: Thoughts in Verse
for the Sundays and Holy Days throughout the Year. Elegantly printed with red borders. 16mo. 2s. 6d. Cheap edition, without the red borders, cloth limp, 1s.; or in paper cover, 6d.

Forming a Volume of "Rivington's Devotional Series."

Also New Editions, forming Volumes of the "Library of Spiritual Works for English Catholics." Small 8vo. 5s. 32mo., cloth limp, 6d.; cloth extra, 1s. [See page 17.]

Private Devotions for School-boys;
with Rules of Conduct. By WILLIAM HENRY, Third Lord Lyttelton. New Edition. 32mo. 6d.

From Morning to Evening : a Book for
Invalids. From the French of M. l'Abbé Henri Perreyve. Translated and adapted by an Associate of the Sisterhood of S. John Baptist, Clewer. Crown 8vo. 5s.

Consoling Thoughts in Sickness.
Edited by HENRY BAILEY, B.D. Small 8vo. 1s. 6d.; or in paper cover, 1s.

A Manual for the Sick; with other
Devotions. By LANCELOT ANDREWES, D.D., sometime Lord Bishop of Winchester. Edited with a Preface by H. P. LIDDON, D.D., Canon of St. Paul's. With Portrait. Third Edition. Large type. 24mo. 2s. 6d.

Sickness; its Trials and Blessings.
Fine Edition. Small 8vo. 3s. 6d. Cheap Edition, 1s. 6d.; or in paper cover, 1s.

Help and Comfort for the Sick Poor.
By the same Author. New Edition. Small 8vo. 1s.

Prayers for the Sick and Dying. By
the same Author. Fourth Edition. Small 8vo. 2s. 6d.

Consolatio; or, Comfort for the
Afflicted. Edited by the Rev. C. E. KENNAWAY. With a Preface by SAMUEL WILBERFORCE, D.D., late Lord Bishop of Winchester. New Edition. Small 8vo. 3s. 6d.

Twenty-one Prayers, composed from the
Psalms, for the Sick and Afflicted. With Hints on the Visitation of the Sick. By the Rev. JAMES SLADE, M.A., Vicar of Bolton. Seventh Edition. 12mo. 3s. 6d.

Thomas à Kempis, Of the Imitation

of Christ. With Red borders. 16mo. 2s. 6d.

Also a Cheap Edition, without the red borders, 1s.; or in paper cover, 6d.

Forming a Volume of "Rivington's Devotional Series."

"*A very beautiful edition. We commend it to the Clergy as an excellent gift-book for teachers and other workers.*"—CHURCH TIMES.

"*This work is a precious relic of mediæval times, and will continue to be valued by every section of the Christian Church.*"—WEEKLY REVIEW.

"*A beautifully printed pocket edition of this marvellous production of a man, who, out of the dark mists of popery, saw so much of experimental religion. Those who are well grounded in evangelical truth may use it with profit.*"—RECORD.

"*A very cheap and handsome edition.*"—ROCK.

"*This new edition is a marvel of cheapness.*"—CHURCH REVIEW.

"*Beautifully printed, and very cheap editions of this long-used handbook of devotion.*"—LITERARY WORLD.

Also a New Translation, forming a Volume of the "Library of Spiritual Works for English Catholics." Small 8vo. 5s. 32mo., cloth limp, 6d.; cloth extra, 1s. [See page 17.]

Introduction to the Devout Life.

From the French of Saint Francis of Sales, Bishop and Prince of Geneva. A New Translation. With red borders. 16mo. 2s. 6d.

Forming a Volume of "Rivington's Devotional Series."

"*A very beautiful edition of S. Francis de Sales' 'Devout Life:' a prettier little edition for binding, type, and paper, of a very great book is not often seen.*"—CHURCH REVIEW.

"*The translation is a good one, and the volume is beautifully got up. It would serve admirably as a gift book to those who are able to appreciate so spiritual a writer as St. Francis.*"—CHURCH TIMES.

"*It has been the food and hope of countless souls ever since its first appearance two centuries and a half ago, and it still ranks with Scupoli's 'Combattimento Spirituale,' and Arvisenet's 'Memoriale Vitæ Sacerdotalis,' as among the very best works of ascetic theology.*"—UNION REVIEW.

"*We should be curious to know by how many different hands 'The Devout Life' of S. Francis de Sales had been translated into English. At any rate, its popularity is so great that Messrs. Rivington have just issued another translation of it. The style is good, and the volume is of a most convenient size.*"—JOHN BULL.

"*This volume will be highly valued. The 'Introduction to the Devout Life' is preceded by a sketch of the life of the author, and a dedicatory prayer of the author is also given.*"—PUBLIC OPINION.

Also a New Translation, forming a Volume of the "Library of Spiritual Works for English Catholics." Small 8vo. 5s. [See page 17.]

The English Poems of George Herbert,

together with his Collection of Proverbs, entitled JACULA PRUDENTUM. With red borders. 16mo. 2s. 6d.

Forming a Volume of "Rivington's Devotional Series."

"*This beautiful little volume will be found specially convenient as a pocket manual. The 'Jacula Prudentum,' or proverbs, deserve to be more widely known than they are at present. In many copies of George Herbert's writings these quaint sayings have been unfortunately omitted.*"—ROCK.

"*George Herbert is too much a household name to require any introduction. It will be sufficient to say that Messrs. Rivington have published a most compact and convenient edition of the poems and proverbs of this illustrious English divine.*"—ENGLISH CHURCHMAN.

"*An exceedingly pretty edition, the most attractive form we have yet seen from this delightful author, as a giftbook.*"—UNION REVIEW.

"*A very beautiful edition of the quaint old English bard. All lovers of the 'Holy' Herbert will be grateful to Messrs. Rivington for the care and pains they have bestowed in supplying them with this and withal convenient copy of poems so well known and so deservedly prized.*"—LONDON QUARTERLY REVIEW.

"*A very tasteful little book, and will doubtless be acceptable to many.*"—RECORD.

"*We commend this little book heartily to our readers. It contains Herbert's English poems and the 'Jacula Prudentum,' in a very neat volume, which does much credit to the publishers; it will, we hope, meet with extensive circulation as a choice giftbook at a moderate price.*"—CHRISTIAN OBSERVER.

A Short and Plain Instruction for the

better Understanding of the Lord's Supper; to which is annexed the Office of the Holy Communion, with proper Helps and Directions. By the Right Rev. THOMAS WILSON, D.D., sometime Lord Bishop of Sodor and Man. Complete Edition, in large type, with rubrics and borders in red. 16mo. 2s. 6d.

Also a Cheap Edition, without the red borders, 1s.; or in paper cover, 6d.

Forming a Volume of "Rivington's Devotional Series."

"*The Messrs. Rivington have published a new and unabridged edition of that deservedly popular work, Bishop Wilson on the Lord's Supper. The edition is here presented in three forms, suited to the various members of the household.*"—PUBLIC OPINION.

"*We cannot withhold the expression of our admiration of the style and elegance in which this work is got up.*"—PRESS AND ST. JAMES' CHRONICLE.

"*A departed Author being dead yet speaketh in a way which will never be out of date; Bishop Wilson on the Lord's Supper, published by Messrs. Rivington, in bindings to suit all tastes and pockets.*"—CHURCH REVIEW.

Waterloo Place, London

The Rule and Exercises of Holy Living.
By the Right Rev. JEREMY TAYLOR, D.D., sometime Bishop of Down and Connor, and Dromore. With red borders. 16mo. 2s. 6d.

Also a Cheap Edition, without the red borders, 1s.

Forming a Volume of "Rivington's Devotional Series."

The Rule and Exercises of Holy Dying.
By the Right Rev. JEREMY TAYLOR, D.D., sometime Bishop of Down and Connor, and Dromore. With red borders. 16mo. 2s. 6d.

Also a Cheap Edition, without the red borders, 1s.

The 'HOLY LIVING' and the 'HOLY DYING' may be had bound together in one Volume, 5s.; or without the red borders, 2s. 6d.

Forming a Volume of "Rivington's Devotional Series."

"*The publishers have done good service by the production of these beautiful editions of works, which will never lose their preciousness to devout Christian spirits. We have only to testify to the good taste, judgment, and care shown in these editions. They are extremely beautiful in typography and in the general getting up.*"—ENGLISH INDEPENDENT.

"*We ought not to conclude our notice of recent devotional books, without mentioning to our readers the above new, elegant, and cheap reprint, which we trust will never be out of date or out of favour in the English branch of the Catholic Church.*"—LITERARY CHURCHMAN.

"*These manuals of piety, written by the pen of the most beautiful writer and the most impressive divine of the English Church, need no commendation from us. They are known to the world, read in all lands, and translated, we have heard, into fifty different languages. For two centuries they have fed the faith of thousands upon thousands of souls, now we trust happy with their God, and perhaps meditating in Heaven with gratitude on their celestial truths, kindled in their souls by a writer who was little short of being inspired.*"—ROCK.

"*These little volumes will be appreciated as presents of inestimable value.*"—PUBLIC OPINION.

A Practical Treatise concerning Evil Thoughts:
wherein their Nature, Origin, and Effect are distinctly considered and explained, with many Useful Rules for restraining and suppressing such Thoughts; suited to the various conditions of Life, and the several tempers of Mankind, more especially of melancholy Persons. By WILLIAM CHILCOT, M.A. New Edition. With red borders. 16mo. 2s. 6d.

Forming a Volume of "Rivington's Devotional Series."

and at 𝕺𝖝𝖋𝖔𝖗𝖉 and 𝕮𝖆𝖒𝖇𝖗𝖎𝖉𝖌𝖊

The Spirit of S. Francis de Sales, Bishop

and Prince of Geneva. Translated from the French by the Author of "The Life of S. Francis de Sales," "A Dominican Artist," &c., &c. Crown 8vo. 6s.

"*S. Francis de Sales, as shown to us by the Bishop of Belley, was clearly as bright and lively a companion as many a sinner of witty reputation. He was a student of human nature on the highest grounds, but he used his knowledge for amusement as well as edification. Naturally we learn this from one of his male friends rather than from his female adorers. This friend is Jean-Pierre Camus, Bishop of Belley, author, we are told, of two hundred books—one only however still known to fame, the Spirit of S. Francis de Sales, which has fairly earned him the title of the ecclesiastical Boswell.*"—SATURDAY REVIEW.

"*An admirable translation of Bishop Camus' well-known collection of that good man's sayings and opinions. . . . . Among the best passages in the book are those on charity, on controversy (at p. 404), on true devotion as exemplified in a right fulfilling of our own vocation, and upon hearing the Word of God; the condemnation at page 41 of those who are always finding fault with preachers is almost identical with George Herbert's stanzas on the same subject. As a whole, we can imagine no more delightful companion than 'The Spirit of S. Francis de Sales,' nor, we may add, a more useful one.*"—PEOPLE'S MAGAZINE.

The Hidden Life of the Soul. From

the French. By the Author of "A Dominican Artist," "Life of Bossuet," &c., &c. New Edition. Small 8vo. 2s. 6d.

Also a Cheap Edition, forming a Volume of the "Library of Spiritual Works for English Catholics." 32mo. Cloth limp, 6d.; cloth extra, 1s. [See page 17.]

"*It well deserves the character given it of being 'earnest and sober,' and not 'sensational.'*"—GUARDIAN.

"*From the French of Jean Nicolas Grou, a pious Priest, whose works teach resignation to the Divine will. He loved, we are told, to inculcate simplicity, freedom from all affectation and unreality, the patience and humility which are too surely grounded in self-knowledge to be surprised at a fall, but withal so allied to confidence in God as to make recovery easy and sure. This is the spirit of the volume which is intended to furnish advice to those who would cultivate a quiet, meek, and childlike spirit.*"—PUBLIC OPINION.

"*There is a wonderful charm about these readings—so calm, so true, so thoroughly Christian. We do not know where they would come amiss. As materials for a consecutive series of meditations for the faithful at a series of early celebrations they would be excellent, or for private reading during Advent or Lent.*"—LITERARY CHURCHMAN.

The Light of the Conscience. By

the Author of "The Hidden Life of the Soul," &c. With an Introduction by the Rev. T. T. CARTER, M.A., Rector of Clewer, Berks. Crown 8vo. 5s.

Devotional Works

Ancient Hymns. From the Roman Breviary. For Domestic Use every Morning and Evening of the Week, and on the Holy Days of the Church. To which are added, Original Hymns, principally of Commemoration and Thanksgiving for Christ's Holy Ordinances. By RICHARD MANT, D.D., sometime Lord Bishop of Down and Connor. New Edition. Small 8vo. 5*s.*

"*Real poetry wedded to words that breathe the purest and the sweetest spirit of Christian devotion. The translations from the old Latin Hymnal are close and faithful renderings.*"—STANDARD.

"*As a Hymn writer Bishop Mant deservedly occupies a prominent place in the esteem of Churchmen, and we doubt not that many will be the readers who will welcome this new edition of his translations and original compositions.*"—ENGLISH CHURCHMAN.

"*A new edition of Bishop Mant's 'Ancient Hymns from the Roman Breviary' forms a handsome little volume, and it is interesting to compare some of these translations with the more modern ones of our own day.*

While we have no hesitation in awarding the palm to the latter, the former are an evidence of the earliest germs of that yearning of the devout mind for something better than Tate and Brady, and which is now so richly supplied."—CHURCH TIMES.

"*This valuable manual will be of great assistance to all compilers of Hymn Books. The translations are graceful, clear, and forcible, and the original hymns deserve the highest praise. Bishop Mant has caught the very spirit of true psalmody, his metre flows musically, and there is a tuneful ring in his verses which especially adapts them for congregational singing.*"—ROCK.

The Mysteries of Mount Calvary. Translated from the Latin of Antonio de Guevara. Edited by the Rev. ORBY SHIPLEY, M.A. Square crown 8vo. 3*s.* 6*d.*

Counsels on Holiness of Life. Translated from the Spanish of "The Sinner's Guide" by Luis de Granada. Edited by the Rev. ORBY SHIPLEY, M.A. Square crown 8vo. 5*s.*

Preparation for Death. Translated from the Italian of Alfonso, Bishop of S. Agatha. Edited by the Rev. ORBY SHIPLEY, M.A. Square crown 8vo. 5*s.*

Examination of Conscience upon Special Subjects. Translated and abridged from the French of Tronson. Edited by the Rev. ORBY SHIPLEY, M.A. Square crown 8vo. 5*s.*

and at Oxford and Cambridge

Faith and Life: Readings for the greater
Holy Days, and the Sundays from Advent to Trinity. Compiled from Ancient Writers. By WILLIAM BRIGHT, D.D., Canon of Christ Church, and Regius Professor of Ecclesiastical History in the University of Oxford. Second Edition. Small 8vo. 5*s*.

Sacra Privata: The Private Meditations
and Prayers of the Right Rev. THOMAS WILSON, D.D., late Lord Bishop of Sodor and Man, accommodated to general use. New Edition, with a Memoir of the Author. 32mo. 1*s*.
Also an Edition in large type. Small 8vo. 2*s*.

Strena Christiana; a Christian New
Year's Gift; or, Brief Exhortations to the Chief Outward Acts of Virtue. Translated from the Latin of Sir Harbottle Grimston, Bart., Member of Parliament, 1640. 32mo. 1*s*. 6*d*.
Or the Latin and English together. 32mo. 2*s*. 6*d*.

Christian Watchfulness, in the Prospect of Sickness, Mourning, and Death.
By JOHN JAMES, D.D., sometime Canon of Peterborough. New Edition. 12mo. 3*s*.

Evangelical Life, as seen in the Example of our Lord Jesus Christ.
By JOHN JAMES, D.D. sometime Canon of Peterborough. Second Edition. 12mo. 7*s*. 6*d*.

Spiritual Life. By JOHN JAMES, D.D.,
sometime Canon of Peterborough. 12mo. 5*s*.

Waterloo Place, London

Morning Notes of Praise. A Series of
Meditations upon the Morning Psalms. Dedicated to the Countess of Cottenham. By LADY CHARLOTTE-MARIA PEPYS. New Edition. Small 8vo. 2s. 6d.

Quiet Moments; a Four Weeks' Course
of Thoughts and Meditations before Evening Prayer and at Sunset. By LADY CHARLOTTE-MARIA PEPYS. New Edition. Small 8vo. 2s. 6d.

A Companion to the Lord's Supper.
By the Plain Man's Friend. Fifth Edition. 18mo. 8d.

A Manual of Devotion, chiefly for the
use of Schoolboys. By the Rev. WILLIAM BAKER, D.D., Head Master of Merchant Taylors' School. With Preface by J. R. WOODFORD, D.D., Lord Bishop of Ely. Crown 16mo. 2s. 6d.

The Good Shepherd; or, Christ the
Pattern, Priest, and Pastor. By the Rev. W. E. HEYGATE, M.A., Rector of Brighstone. New Edition, Revised. Small 8vo. 3s. 6d.

and at 𝔒xford and Cambridge

4. Parish Work.

The Book of Church Law. Being an
Exposition of the Legal Rights and Duties of the Clergy and Laity of the Church of England. By the Rev. JOHN HENRY BLUNT, M.A., F.S.A. Revised by WALTER G. F. PHILLIMORE, B.C.L., Barrister-at-Law, and Chancellor of the Diocese of Lincoln. Second Edition, thoroughly revised and brought down to the present time. Crown 8vo. 7s. 6d.

CONTENTS.

BOOK I.—THE CHURCH AND ITS LAWS.—The Constitutional Status of the Church of England—The Law of the Church of England—The Administration of Church Law.

BOOK II.—THE MINISTRATIONS OF THE CHURCH.—Holy Baptism—Confirmation—The Holy Communion—Divine Service in General—Holy Matrimony—The Churching of Women—The Visitation of the Sick—The Practice of Confession—The Burial of the Dead.

BOOK III.—THE PAROCHIAL CLERGY.—Holy Orders—Licensed Curates—The Cure of Souls.

BOOK IV.—PAROCHIAL LAY OFFICERS.—Churchwardens—Church Trustees—Parish Clerks, Sextons and Beadles—Vestries.

BOOK V.—CHURCHES AND CHURCHYARDS.—The Acquisition of Churches and Churchyards as Ecclesiastical Property—Churches and Ecclesiastical Persons—Churches and Secular Persons.

BOOK VI.—THE ENDOWMENTS OF THE PAROCHIAL CLERGY.—Incomes—Parsonage Houses—The Sequestration of Benefices.

APPENDIX.—The Canons of 1603 and 1865—The Church Discipline Act of 1840—The Benefices Resignation Act of 1871—The Ecclesiastical Dilapidations Act of 1871—The Sequestration Act of 1871—The Public Worship Regulation Act of 1874—Index.

" *We have tested this work on various points of a crucial character, and have found it very accurate and full in its information. It embodies the results of the most recent Acts of the Legislature on the clerical profession and the rights of the laity.*"—STANDARD.

" *Already in our leading columns we have directed attention to Messrs. Blunt and Phillimore's ' Book of Church Law,' as an excellent manual for ordinary use. It is a book which should stand on every clergyman's shelves ready for use when any legal matter arises about which its possessor is in doubt. . . . It is to be hoped that the authorities at our Theological Colleges sufficiently recognize the value of a little legal knowledge on the part of the clergy to recommend this book to their students. It would serve admirably as the text-book for a set of lectures.*"—CHURCH TIMES.

Waterloo Place, London

Directorium Pastorale. The Principles

and Practice of Pastoral Work in the Church of England. By the Rev. JOHN HENRY BLUNT, M.A., F.S.A., Editor of "The Annotated Book of Common Prayer," &c., &c. Third Edition, revised. Crown 8vo. 7s. 6d.

"*This is the third edition of a work which has become deservedly popular as the best extant exposition of the principles and practice of the pastoral work in the Church of England. Its hints and suggestions are based on practical experience, and it is further recommended by the majority of our Bishops at the ordination of priests and deacons.*"—STANDARD.

"*Its practical usefulness to the parochial clergy is proved by the acceptance it has already received at their hands, and no faithful parish priest, who is working in real earnest for the extension of spiritual instruction amongst all classes of his flock, will rise from the perusal of its pages without having obtained some valuable hints as to the best mode of bringing home our Church's system to the hearts of his people.*"—NATIONAL CHURCH.

Priest and Parish. By the Rev. HARRY

JONES, M.A., Rector of St. George's-in-the-East, London. Square crown 8vo. 6s. 6d.

Ars Pastoria. By FRANK PARNELL, M.A.,

Rector of Oxtead, near Godstone. Small 8vo. 2s.

Instructions for the Use of Candidates

for Holy Orders, and of the Parochial Clergy; with Acts of Parliament relating to the same, and Forms proposed to be used. By CHRISTOPHER HODGSON, M.A., Secretary to the Governors of Queen Anne's Bounty. Ninth Edition. 8vo. 16s.

Post-Mediæval Preachers: Some Ac-

count of the most Celebrated Preachers of the 15th, 16th, and 17th Centuries; with Outlines of their Sermons, and Specimens of their style. By the Rev. S. BARING-GOULD, M.A. Post 8vo. 7s.

and at Oxford and Cambridge

Flowers and Festivals; or, Directions

for the Floral Decoration of Churches. By W. A. BARRETT, Mus. Bac., Oxon., of St. Paul's Cathedral. With Coloured Illustrations. Second Edition. Square 16mo. 5s.

The Chorister's Guide. By W. A. BAR-

RETT, Mus. Bac., Oxon, of St. Paul's Cathedral. Second Edition. Crown 8vo. 2s. 6d.

". . . One of the most useful books of instructions for choristers—and, we may add, choral singers generally—that has ever emanated from the musical press. . . . Mr. Barrett's teaching is not only conveyed to his readers with the consciousness of being master of his subject, but he employs words terse and clear, so that his meaning may be promptly caught by the neophyte. . . ."—ATHENÆUM.

"A nicely graduated, clear, and excellent introduction to the duties of a chorister."—STANDARD.

"It seems clear and precise enough to serve its end."—EXAMINER.

"A useful manual for giving boys such a practical and technical knowledge of music as shall enable them to sing both with confidence and precision."—CHURCH HERALD.

"In this little volume we have a manual long called for by the requirements of church music. In a series of thirty-two lessons it gives, with an admirable conciseness, and an equally observable completeness, all that is necessary a chorister should be taught out of a book, and a great deal calculated to have a value as bearing indirectly upon his actual practice in singing."—MUSICAL STANDARD.

"We can highly recommend the present able manual."—EDUCATIONAL TIMES.

"A very useful manual, not only for choristers, or rather those who may aim at becoming choristers, but for others, who wish to enter upon the study of music."—ROCK.

"The work will be found of singular utility by those who have to instruct choirs."—CHURCH TIMES.

"A most grateful contribution to the agencies for improving our Services. It is characterised by all that clearness in combination with conciseness of style which has made 'Flowers and Festivals' so universally admired."—TORONTO HERALD.

Church Organs: their Position and Con-

struction. With an Appendix containing some Account of the Mediæval Organ Case still existing at Old Radnor, South Wales. By FREDERICK HEATHCOTE SUTTON, M.A., Vicar of Theddingworth. With Illustrations. Folio. 6s. 6d.

Notes on Church Organs: their Position

and the Materials used in their Construction. By C. K. K. BISHOP. With Illustrations. Small 4to. 6s.

𝕬𝖆𝖙𝖊𝖗𝖑𝖔𝖔 𝕻𝖑𝖆𝖈𝖊, 𝕷𝖔𝖓𝖉𝖔𝖓

Stones of the Temple; or, Lessons

from the Fabric and Furniture of the Church. By WALTER FIELD, M.A., F.S.A., Vicar of Godmersham. With numerous Illustrations. New Edition. Crown 8vo. 7s. 6d.

"*Any one who wishes for simple information on the subjects of Church-architecture and furniture, cannot do better than consult 'Stones of the Temple.' Mr. Field modestly disclaims any intention of supplanting the existing regular treatises, but his book shows an amount of research, and a knowledge of what he is talking about, which make it practically useful as well as pleasant. The woodcuts are numerous, and some of them very pretty.*"—GRAPHIC.

"*A very charming book, by the Rev. Walter Field, who was for years Secretary of one of the leading Church Societies. Mr. Field has a loving reverence for the beauty of the* domus mansionalis Dei, *as the old law books called the Parish Church. . . . Thoroughly sound in Church feeling, Mr. Field has chosen the medium of a tale to embody real incidents illustrative of the various portions of his subject. There is no attempt at elaboration of the narrative, which, indeed, is rather a string of anecdotes than a story, but each chapter brings home to the mind its own lesson, and each is illustrated with some very interesting engravings. . . . The work will properly command a hearty reception from Churchmen. The footnotes are occasionally most valuable, and are always pertinent, and the text is sure to be popular with young folks for Sunday reading.*"—STANDARD.

"*Mr. Field's chapters on brasses, chancel screens, crosses, encaustic tiles, mural paintings, porches and pavements, are agreeably written, and people with a turn for Ritualism will no doubt find them edifying. The illustrations of Church-architecture and Church ornaments are very attractive.*"—PALL MALL GAZETTE.

"'*Stones of the Temple' is a grave book, the result of antiquarian, or rather ecclesiological, tastes and of devotional feelings. We can recommend it to young people of both sexes, and it will not disappoint the most learned among them. . . . Mr. Field has brought together, from well known authorities, a considerable mass of archæological information, which will interest the readers he especially addresses.*"—ATHENÆUM.

"*Very appropriate as a Christmas present, is an elegant and instructive book. . . . A full and clear account of the meaning and history of the several parts of the fabric and of the furniture of the Church. It is illustrated with a number of carefully drawn pictures, sometimes of entire churches, sometimes of remarkable monuments, windows, or wall paintings. We may add that the style of the commentary, which is cast in the form of a dialogue between a parson and some of his parishioners, and hangs together by a slight thread of story, is quiet and sensible, and free from exaggeration or intolerance.*"—GUARDIAN.

A Handy Book on the Ecclesiastical

Dilapidations Act, 1871. With the Amendment Act, 1872. By EDWARD G. BRUTON, F.R.I.B.A., Diocesan Surveyor, Oxford. With Analytical Index and Precedent Forms. Second Edition. Crown 8vo. 5s.

---

and at 𝔒xford and Cambridge

The Church Builder: a Quarterly Journal of Church Extension in England and Wales. Published in connexion with "The Incorporated Church Building Society." 14 Annual Volumes. With Illustrations. Crown 8vo. 1s. 6d. each. [Sold separately.

List of Charities, General and Diocesan, for the Relief of the Clergy, their Widows and Families. New Edition. Small 8vo. 3s.

5. The Church and Doctrine.

The Holy Catholic Church; its Divine
Ideal, Ministry, and Institutions. A short Treatise. With a Catechism on each Chapter, forming a Course of Methodical Instruction on the subject. By EDWARD MEYRICK GOULBURN, D.D., Dean of Norwich. Second Edition. Crown 8vo. 6s. 6d.

CONTENTS.

What the Church is, and when and how it was founded—Duty of the Church towards those who hold to the Apostles' doctrine, in separation from the Apostles' fellowship—The Unity of the Church, and its Disruption—The Survey of Zion's towers, bulwarks, and palaces—The Institution of the Ministry, and its relation to the Church—The Holy Eucharist at its successive stages—On the powers of the Church in Council—The Church presenting, exhibiting, and defending the Truth—The Church guiding into and illustrating the Truth—On the Prayer-Book as a Commentary on the Bible—Index.

"*Dr. Goulburn has conferred a great boon on the Church of England by the treatise before us, which vindicates her claim as a branch of the Catholic Church on the allegiance of her children, setting forth as he does, with singular precision and power, the grounds of her title-deeds, and the Christian character of her doctrine and discipline.*"—STANDARD.

"*His present book would have been used for an educational book even if he had not invited men to make that use of it by appending a catechism to each particular chapter, and thus founding a course of methodical instruction upon his text. We have not yet come across any better book for giving to Dissenters or to such inquirers as hold fast to Holy Scripture. It is, we need scarcely say, steeped in Scripturalness, and full of bright and suggestive interpretations of particular texts.*"—ENGLISH CHURCHMAN.

"*Must prove highly useful, not only to young persons, but to the very large class, both Churchmen and Dissenters, who are painfully ignorant of what the Catholic Church really is, and of the peculiar and fixed character of her institutions.*"—ROCK.

"*The catechetical questions and answers at the end of each chapter will be useful both for teachers and learners, and the side-notes at the head of the paragraphs are very handy.*"—CHURCH TIMES.

"*It contains a great deal of instructive matter, especially in the catechisms —or, as they might be called, dialogues —and is instinct with a spirit at once temperate and uncompromising. It is a good book for all who wish to understand, neither blindly asserting it nor being half ashamed of it, the position of a loyal member of the English Church.*"—GUARDIAN.

---

and at Oxford and Cambridge

Dictionary of Doctrinal and Historical

Theology. By Various Writers. Edited by the Rev. JOHN HENRY BLUNT, M.A., F.S.A., Editor of the "Annotated Book of Common Prayer," &c., &c. Second Edition, Imperial 8vo. 42s.; or in half-morocco, 52s. 6d.

"*Taken as a whole the articles are the work of practised writers, and well-informed and solid theologians. .... We know no book of its size and bulk which supplies the information here given at all; far less which supplies it in an arrangement so accessible, with a completeness of information so thorough, and with an ability in the treatment of profound subjects so great. Dr. Hook's most useful volume is a work of high calibre, but it is the work of a single mind. We have here a wider range of thought from a greater variety of sides. We have here also the work of men who evidently know what they write about, and are somewhat more profound (to say the least) than the writers of the current Dictionaries of Sects and Heresies.*"—GUARDIAN.

"*Thus it will be obvious that it takes a very much wider range than any undertaking of the same kind in our language; and that to those of our clergy who have not the fortune to spend in books, and would not have the leisure to use them if they possessed them, it will be the most serviceable and reliable substitute for a large library we can think of. And in many cases, while keeping strictly within its province as a Dictionary, it contrives to be marvellously suggestive of thought and reflections, which a serious-minded man will take with him and ponder over for his own elaboration and future use. We trust most sincerely that the book may be largely used. For a present to a Clergyman on his ordination, or from a parishioner to his pastor, it would be most appropriate. It may indeed be called 'a box of tools for a working clergyman.'*"—LITERARY CHURCHMAN.

"*Seldom has an English work of equal magnitude been so permeated with Catholic instincts, and at the same time seldom has a work on theology been kept so free from the drift of rhetorical incrustation. Of course, it is not meant that all these remarks apply in their full extent to every article. In a great Dictionary there are compositions, as in a great house there are vessels, of various kinds. Some of these at a future day may be replaced by others more substantial in their build, more proportionate in their outline, and more elaborate in their detail. But admitting all this, the whole remains a home to which the student will constantly recur, sure to find spacious chambers, substantial furniture, and (which is most important) no stinted light.*"—CHURCH REVIEW.

"*Within the sphere it has marked out for itself, no equally useful book of reference exists in English for the elucidation of theological problems. ... Entries which display much care, research, and judgment in compilation, and which will make the task of the parish priest who is brought face to face with any of the practical questions which they involve far easier than has been hitherto. The very fact that the utterances are here and there somewhat more guarded and hesitating than quite accords with our judgment, is a gain in so far as it protects the work from the charge of inculcating extreme views, and will thus secure its admission in many places where moderation is accounted the crowning grace.*"—CHURCH TIMES.

"*It will be found of admirable service to all students of theology, as advancing and maintaining the Church's views on all subjects as fall within the range of fair argument and inquiry. It is not often that a work of so comprehensive and so profound a nature is marked to the very end by so many signs of wide and careful research, sound criticism, and well-founded and well-expressed belief.*"—STANDARD.

Waterloo Place, London

Dictionary of Sects, Heresies, Ecclesiastical Parties and Schools of Religious Thought. By Various Writers. Edited by the Rev. JOHN HENRY BLUNT, M.A., F.S.A., Editor of the "Dictionary of Doctrinal and Historical Theology," the "Annotated Book of Common Prayer," &c., &c. Imperial 8vo. 36s.; or in half-morocco, 48s.

"*Taken as a whole, we doubt not that the Dictionary will prove a useful work of reference; and it may claim to give in reasonable compass a mass of information respecting many religious schools knowledge of which could previously only be acquired from amid a host of literature. The articles are written with great fairness, and in many cases display careful scholarly work.*"—ATHENÆUM.

"*A very comprehensive and bold undertaking, and is certainly executed with a sufficient amount of ability and knowledge to entitle the book to rank very high in point of utility.*"—GUARDIAN.

"*That this is a work of some learning and research is a fact which soon becomes obvious to the reader.*"—SPECTATOR.

"*A whole library is condensed into this admirable volume. All authorities are named, and an invaluable index is supplied.*"—NOTES AND QUERIES.

"*We have tested it rigidly, and in almost every instance we have been satisfied with the account given under the name of sects, heresy, or ecclesiastical party.*"—JOHN BULL.

"*After all deductions, it is the fullest and most trustworthy book of the kind that we possess. The quantity of information it presents in a convenient and accessible form is enormous, and having once appeared, it becomes indispensable to the theological student.*"—CHURCH TIMES.

"*It has considerable value as a copious work of reference, more especially since a list of authorities is in most cases supplied.*"—EXAMINER.

The Doctrine of the Church of England, as stated in Ecclesiastical Documents set forth by Authority of Church and State, in the Reformation Period between 1536 and 1662. Edited by the Rev. JOHN HENRY BLUNT, M.A., F.S.A., Editor of the "Dictionary of Doctrinal and Historical Theology," the "Annotated Book of Common Prayer," &c. &c. 8vo. 7s. 6d.

The Position of the Celebrant at the Holy Communion, as ruled by the Purchas Judgment, considered in a Letter to the Lord Bishop of Winchester. By MORTON SHAW, M.A., Rector of Rougham, Suffolk, Rural Dean. Third Edition. 8vo. 5s.

and at Oxford and Cambridge

The Principal Ecclesiastical Judg-
ments delivered in the Court of Arches, 1867-1875. By the
Right Hon. Sir ROBERT PHILLIMORE, D.C.L. 8vo. 12s.

Thirty-two Years of the Church of
England, 1842-1875 : The Charges of Archdeacon SINCLAIR.
Edited by WILLIAM SINCLAIR, M.A., Prebendary of Chichester,
Rector of Pulborough, late Vicar of S. George's, Leeds. With
a Preface by ARCHIBALD CAMPBELL TAIT, D.D., Archbishop
of Canterbury, and a Historical Introduction by ROBERT
CHARLES JENKINS, M.A., Hon. Canon of Canterbury, Rector
and Vicar of Lyminge. 8vo.

The Holy Angels : Their Nature and
Employments, as recorded in the Word of God. Small 8vo.
6s.

A Plain Statement of the Evidence of
Scripture and Tradition on Church Government. By the Rev.
JOHN MITCHELL, M.A. Small 8vo. 2s.

Prophecies and the Prophetic Spirit
in the Christian Era : an Historical Essay. By JOHN J.
IGN. VON DÖLLINGER, D.D., D.C.L. Translated, with
Introduction, Notes, and Appendices, by the Rev. ALFRED
PLUMMER, M.A., Master of University College, Durham,
late Fellow of Trinity College, Oxford. 8vo. 10s. 6d.

Lectures on the Reunion of the
Churches. By JOHN J. IGN. VON DÖLLINGER, D.D., D.C.L.
Authorized Translation, with Preface by HENRY NUTCOMBE
OXENHAM, M.A., late Scholar of Balliol College, Oxford.
Crown 8vo. 5s.

Apostolical Succession in the Church

of England. By the Rev. ARTHUR W. HADDAN, B.D., late Rector of Barton-on-the-Heath. 8vo. 12s.

"*Thoroughly well written, clear and forcible in style, and fair in tone. It cannot but render valuable service in placing the claims of the Church in their true light before the English public.*"—GUARDIAN.

"*Among the many standard theological works devoted to this important subject Mr. Haddan's will hold a high place.*"—STANDARD.

"*We should be glad to see the volume widely circulated and generally read.*"—JOHN BULL.

"*A weighty and valuable treatise, and we hope that the study of its sound and well-reasoned pages will do much to fix the importance, and the full meaning of the doctrine in question, in the minds of Church people. . . .*

We hope that our extracts will lead our readers to study Mr. Haddan for themselves."—LITERARY CHURCHMAN.

"*This is not only a very able and carefully written treatise upon the doctrine of Apostolical Succession, but it is also a calm yet noble vindication of the validity of the Anglican Orders: it well sustains the brilliant reputation which Mr. Haddan left behind him at Oxford, and it supplements his other profound historical researches in ecclesiastical matters. This book will remain for a long time the classic work upon English Orders.*"—CHURCH REVIEW.

"*A very temperate, but a very well reasoned book.*"—WESTMINSTER REVIEW.

The Civil Power in its Relations to the

Church; considered with Special Reference to the Court of Final Ecclesiastical Appeal in England. By the Rev. JAMES WAYLAND JOYCE, M.A., Prebendary of Hereford, and Examining Chaplain to the Bishop of Hereford. 8vo. 10s. 6d.

Defence of the English Ordinal, with

some Observations upon Spiritual Jurisdiction and the Power of the Keys. By the Rev. W. R. CHURTON, M.A., Fellow of King's College, Cambridge, and Honorary Canon of Rochester Cathedral. 8vo. 3s.

The Religion, Discipline, and Rites of

the Church of England. Written at the Instance of Edward Hyde, Earl of Clarendon. By JOHN COSIN, sometime Bishop of Durham. Now first published in English. By the Rev. FREDERICK MEYRICK, M.A. Small 8vo. 1s.

---

and at Oxford and Cambridge

Eight Lectures on the Miracles; being
the Bampton Lectures for 1865. By J. B. MOZLEY, D.D., Regius Professor of Divinity, and Canon of Christ Church, Oxford. Third Edition. Crown 8vo. 7s. 6d.

"*There is great brightness and beauty in many of the images in which the author condenses the issues of his arguments. And many passages are marked by that peculiar kind of eloquence which comes with the force of close and vigorous thinking; passages which slime-like steal through their very temper, and which are instinct with a controlled energy, that melts away all ruggedness of language. There can be no question that, in the deeper qualities of a scientific theology, the book is thoroughly worthy of the highest reputation which had been gained by Mr. Mozley's previous writings.*"—CONTEMPORARY REVIEW.

"*Mr. Mozley's Bampton Lectures are an example, and a very fine one, of a mode of theological writing which is characteristic of the Church of England, and almost peculiar to it. The distinguishing features, a combination of intense seriousness with a self-restrained, severe calmness, and of very vigorous and wide-ranging reasoning on the realities of the case. . . . . . Mr. Mozley's book belongs to that class of writings of which Butler may be taken as the type. It is strong, genuine argument about difficult matters fairly facing what is difficult, fairly trying to grapple, not with what appears the gist and strong point of a question, but with what really and at bottom is the knot of it.*"—TIMES.

The Happiness of the Blessed con-
sidered as to the Particulars of their State: their Recognition of each other in that State: and its Differences of Degrees. To which are added Musings on the Church and her Services. By RICHARD MANT, D.D., sometime Lord Bishop of Down and Connor. New Edition. Small 8vo. 3s. 6d.

'*A welcome republication of a treatise once highly valued, and which can never lose its value. Many of our readers already know the fulness and discrimination with which the author treats his subject, which must be one of the most delightful topics of meditation to all whose hearts are where the only true treasure is, and particularly to those who are entering upon the evening of life.*"—CHURCH REVIEW.

"*The value of this book needs not to be referred to, its standard character having been for many years past established. The edition in which it reappears has evidently been carefully prepared, and will be the means of making it more generally known.*"— BELL'S MESSENGER.

"*All recognise the authority of the command to set the affections on things above, and such works as the one now before us will be found helpful towards this good end. We are, therefore, sincerely glad that Messrs. Rivington have brought out a new edition of Bishop Mant's valuable treatise.*"— RECORD.

"*This beautiful and devotional treatise, which it is impossible to read without feeling a more deepened interest in the eternal blessedness which awaits the true servants of our God, concludes very appropriately with 'Musings on the Church and her Services,' which we cordially recommend to our readers.*" —ROCK.

Out of the Body. A Scriptural Inquiry.
By the Rev. JAMES S. POLLOCK, M.A., Incumbent of S. Alban's, Birmingham. Crown 8vo. 5s.

CONTENTS.

Introduction—Scope of the Inquiry—The Presentiment—The Anticipation—The Departure—The Life of the Body—The Life of the Spirit—Dream-Life—The Spirit-World—Spirit-Groups—Helping one another—Limits of Communication—Spiritual Manifestations.

"*We have read this book with interest. . . We esteem the honesty with which it is evidently written, and we admire the courage which the author has shown in searching the Bible for evidences as to the destination of departed spirits, and in accepting such evidences as he has found.*"—BIRMINGHAM MORNING NEWS.

"*The writer discusses with considerable ability, and in a devout and reverent frame of mind.*"—SPIRITUAL MAGAZINE.

"*This is a curious, thoughtful, and interesting little book, in which the author endeavours to ascertain and to define the relations of living men as regards their communication with the spirits of those whom we call dead, as authorised by the words and teaching of Holy Scripture. . . . Will be very welcome to a host of readers on either side of the disputed ground, and cannot fail to be of lasting interest and profit to all candid students.*"—STANDARD.

The Origin and Development of Religious Belief.
By the Rev. S. BARING-GOULD, M.A., Author of "Curious Myths of the Middle Ages," &c.

Vol. I. MONOTHEISM and POLYTHEISM. Second Edition. 8vo. 15s.

Vol. II. CHRISTIANITY. 8vo. 15s.

"*The ability which Mr. Baring-Gould displays in the treatment of a topic which branches out in so many directions, and requires such precise handling, is apparent. His pages abound with the results of large reading and calm reflection. The man of culture, thought, philosophic cast, is mirrored in the entire argument. The book is sound and healthy in tone. It excites the reader's interest, and brightens the path of inquiry opened to his view. The language, too, is appropriate, neat, lucid, often happy, sometimes wonderfully terse and vigorous.*"—ATHENÆUM.

"*Mr. Baring-Gould has undertaken a great and ambitious work. And no one can deny that he possesses some eminent qualifications for this great work. He has a wealth of erudition of the most varied description, especially in those particular regions of mediæval legend and Teutonic mythology which are certain to make large contributions to the purpose he has in hand. It is a contribution to religious thought of very high value.*"—GUARDIAN.

"*Mr. Baring-Gould's work, from the importance of its subject and the lucid force of its expositions, as well as from the closeness of argument and copiousness of illustration with which its comprehensive views are treated, is entitled to attentive study, and will repay the reader by amusement and instruction.*"—MORNING POST.

"*Our space warns us that we are attempting in vain to compress into a few columns the contents of four hundred pages of a work which has had few equals for brilliancy, learning, and point in this department of literature. We therefore conclude by recommending the volume itself to all students of mind and theology.*"—CHURCH TIMES.

Our Mother Church: being Simple Talk
on High Topics. By ANNE MERCIER. New Edition. Small 8vo. 3s. 6d.

"*We have rarely come across a book dealing with an old subject in a healthier and, as far as may be, more original manner, while yet thoroughly practical. It is intended for and admirably adapted to the use of girls. Thoroughly reverent in its tone, and bearing in every page marks of learned research, it is yet easy of comprehension, and explains ecclesiastical terms with the accuracy of a lexicon without the accompanying dulness. It is to be hoped that the book will attain to the large circulation it justly merits.*"—JOHN BULL.

"*We have never seen a book for girls of its class which commends itself to us more particularly. The author, who is the wife of an earnest parish priest of the Anglican school, near London, calls her work 'simple talk on great subjects,' and calls it by a name that describes it almost as completely as we could do in a longer notice than we can spare the volume. Here are the headings of the chapters:—*

'*The Primitive Church*,' '*Primitive Places and Modes of Worship*,' '*The Early English Church*,' '*The Monastic Orders*,' '*The Friars*,' '*A Review of Church History*,' '*The Prayer Book*,' (*four chapters*), '*Symbolism*,' '*Church Architecture*,' '*Windows and Bells*,' '*Church Music*,' '*Church Work*.' *No one can fail to comprehend the beautifully simple, devout, and appropriate language in which Mrs. Mercier embodies what she has to say; and for the facts with which she deals she has taken good care to have their accuracy assured.*"—STANDARD.

"*The plan of this pleasant-looking book is excellent It is a kind of Mrs. Markham on the Church of England, written especially for girls, and we shall not be surprised to find it become a favourite in schools. It is really a conversational hand-book to the English Church's history, doctrine, and ritual, compiled by a very diligent reader from some of the best modern Anglican sources.*"—ENGLISH CHURCHMAN.

A Selection from the Spiritual Letters
of S. Francis de Sales, Bishop and Prince of Geneva. Translated by the Author of "Life of S. Francis de Sales," "A Dominican Artist," &c. &c. Crown 8vo. 6s.

"*It is a collection of epistolary correspondence of rare interest and excellence. With those who have read the Life, there cannot but have been a strong desire to know more of so beautiful a character.*"—CHURCH HERALD.

"*A few months back we had the pleasure of welcoming the Life of S. Francis de Sales. Here is the promised sequel:—the 'Selection from his Spiritual Letters' then announced:— and a great boon it will be to many. The Letters are addressed to people of all sorts:—to men and to women:—to laity and to ecclesiastics, to people living in the world, or at court, and to the inmates of Religious Houses. We hope that with our readers it may be totally needless to urge such a volume on their notice.*"—LITERARY CHURCHMAN.

Also a Cheap Edition, forming a Volume of the "Library of Spiritual Works for English Catholics." 32mo., cloth limp, 6d.; cloth extra, 1s. [See page 17.]

Church and Doctrine

The Argument Delivered before the
Judicial Committee of the Privy Council. By ARCHIBALD JOHN STEPHENS, LL.D., one of Her Majesty's Counsel in the case of THOMAS BYARD SHEPPARD against WILLIAM EARLY BENNETT, Clerk. With an Appendix containing their Lordships' Judgment. 8vo. 9s.

St. John Chrysostom's Liturgy. Translated by H. C. ROMANOFF, Author of "Sketches of the Rites and Customs of the Greco-Russian Church," &c. With Illustrations. Square crown 8vo. 4s. 6d.

The Intermediate State of the Soul
between Death and the Resurrection. A Sermon preached at the Church of All Saints, Windsor. By CHR. WORDSWORTH, D.D., Bishop of Lincoln. 18mo. 1s.

Union with Rome; or, Is the Church
of Rome the Babylon of the Apocalypse? By CHR. WORDSWORTH, D.D., Bishop of Lincoln. Eighth Edition. 1s.

Report of the Proceedings at the Re-
union Conference held at Bonn, September 1874. With a Preface by HENRY PARRY LIDDON, D.D., D.C.L., Canon of St. Paul's, and Ireland Professor of Exegesis in the University of Oxford. Small 8vo. 3s. 6d.

Dogmatic Faith: an Inquiry into the
Relation subsisting between Revelation and Dogma. Being the Bampton Lectures for 1867. By EDWARD GARBETT, M.A., Incumbent of Christ Church, Surbiton. New Edition. Crown 8vo. 5s.

and at Oxford and Cambridge

Letters from Rome on the Council.
By QUIRINUS. Reprinted from the "Allgemeine Zeitung." Authorized Translation. Crown 8vo. 12s.

The Pope and the Council. By JANUS.
Authorized Translation from the German. Fourth Edition. Crown 8vo. 7s. 6d.

A Vicar's View of Church Patronage.
By the Rev. J. GODSON, M.A., Vicar of Ashby Folville, in the Diocese of Peterborough. Small 8vo. 2s.

The Thirty-nine Articles of the Church
of England explained in a Series of Lectures. By the Rev. R. W. JELF, D.D., late Canon of Christ Church, Oxford, and sometime Principal of King's College, London. Edited by the Rev. J. R. KING, M.A., Vicar of St. Peter's-in-the-East, Oxford, and formerly Fellow and Tutor of Merton College. 8vo. 15s.

6. Sermons.

Some Elements of Religion. Lent
Lectures. By HENRY PARRY LIDDON, D.D., D.C.L., Canon of St. Paul's, and Ireland Professor of Exegesis in the University of Oxford. Second Edition. Crown 8vo. 5s.

CONTENTS.

The Idea of Religion—God, the Object of Religion—The Subject of Religion, the Soul—The Obstacle to Religion, Sin—Prayer, the Characteristic action of Religion—The Mediator, the Guarantee of Religious Life.

The Divinity of our Lord and Saviour
Jesus Christ. Being the Bampton Lectures for 1866. By HENRY PARRY LIDDON, D.D., D.C.L., Canon of St. Paul's, and Ireland Professor of Exegesis in the University of Oxford. Seventh Edition. Crown 8vo. 5s.

Sermons Preached before the University
of Oxford. By HENRY PARRY LIDDON, D.D., D.C.L., Canon of St. Paul's, and Ireland Professor of Exegesis in the University of Oxford. Sixth Edition. Crown 8vo. 5s.

CONTENTS.

God and the Soul—The Law of Progress—The Honour of Humanity—The Freedom of the Spirit—Immortality—Humility and Action—The Conflict of Faith with undue Exaltation of Intellect—Lessons of the Holy Manger—The Divine Victim—The Risen Life—Our Lord's Ascension, the Church's Gain—Faith in a Holy Ghost—The Divine Indwelling a motive to Holiness.

and at Oxford and Cambridge

The Life of Justification. A Series of
Lectures delivered in Substance at All Saints', Margaret Street. By the Rev. GEORGE BODY, B.A., Rector of Kirkby Misperton. Fourth Edition. Crown 8vo. 4s. 6d.

CONTENTS.

Justification the Want of Humility—Christ our Justification—Union with Christ the Condition of Justification—Conversion and Justification—The Life of Justification—The Progress and End of Justification.

"*On the whole we have rarely met with a more clear, intelligible and persuasive statement of the truth as regards the important topics on which the volume treats. Sermon II. in particular, will strike every one by its eloquence and beauty, but we scarcely like to specify it, lest in praising it we should seem to disparage the other portions of this admirable little work.*"—CHURCH TIMES.

"*These discourses show that their author's position is due to something more and higher than mere fluency, gesticulation, and flexibility of voice. He appears as having drunk deeply at the fountain of St. Augustine, and as understanding how to translate the burning words of that mighty genius into the current language of to-day.*"—UNION REVIEW.

"*There is real power in these sermons:—power, real power, and plenty of it. . . . There is such a moral veraciousness about him, such a profound and over-mastering belief that Christ has proved a bonâ-fide cure for unholiness, and such an intensity of eagerness to lead others to seek and profit by that means of attaining the true sanctity which alone can enter Heaven—that we wonder not at the crowds which hang upon his preaching, nor at the success of his fervid appeals to the human conscience. If any one doubts our verdict, let him buy this volume. No one will regret its perusal.*"—LITERARY CHURCHMAN.

The Life of Temptation. A Course of
Lectures delivered in Substance at St. Peter's, Eaton Square; also at All Saints', Margaret Street. By the Rev. GEORGE BODY, B.A., Rector of Kirkby Misperton. Third Edition. Crown 8vo. 4s. 6d.

CONTENTS.

The Leading into Temptation—The Rationale of Temptation—Why we are Tempted—Safety in Temptation—With Jesus in Temptation—The End of Temptation.

"*Regeneration and conversion seem here to occupy their proper places in the Christian economy, and the general subject of temptation is worked out with considerable ability.*"—CHURCH TIMES.

"*This is another volume of simple, earnest, soul-stirring words, dealing with the mysteries of Christian experience.*"—LONDON QUARTERLY REVIEW.

"*A collection of sermons, pious, earnest, and eloquent.*"—ENGLISH CHURCHMAN.

Sermons on the Epistles and Gospels

for the Sundays and Holy Days throughout the Year. By the Rev. ISAAC WILLIAMS, B.D., Author of a "Devotional Commentary on the Gospel Narrative." New Edition. 2 Vols. Crown 8vo. 5s. each. Sold separately.

CONTENTS OF VOL. I.

The King of Salem—The Scriptures bearing Witness—The Church bearing Witness—The Spirit bearing Witness—The Adoption of Sons—Love strong as Death—The Love which passeth Knowledge—Of such is the Kingdom of Heaven—The Spirit of Adoption—The Old and the New Man—The Day Star in the Heart—Obedience the best Sacrifice—The Meekness and Gentleness of Christ—The Faith that overcometh the World—Our Refuge in Public Troubles—Light and Safety in Love—The Great Manifestation—Perseverance found in Humility—Bringing forth Fruit with Patience—The most excellent Gift—The Call to Repentance—The accepted Time—Perseverance in Prayer—The Unclean Spirit returning—The Penitent refreshed—Our Life in the Knowledge of God—The Mind of Christ—The Triumph of the Cross—The Man of Sorrows—The Great Sacrifice—The Memorial of the Great Sacrifice—The Fulfilment—Buried with Christ—The Power of Christ risen—Walking in Newness of Life—Belief in the Resurrection of Christ—The Faith that overcometh the World—Following the Lamb of God—A little while—The Giver of all Good—Requisites of effectual Prayer—Ascending with Christ—The Days of Expectation—They shall walk with Me in White—The Holy Spirit and Baptism—Let all Things be done in order.

CONTENTS OF VOL. II.

The Door opened in Heaven—Love the mark of God's Children—The Gospel a Feast of Love—The Lost Sheep—Mercy the best preparation for Judgment—The peaceable ordering of the World—Brotherly Love and the Life in Christ—The Bread which God giveth—By their Fruits ye shall know them—Looking forward, or Divine Covetousness—The Day of Visitation—The Prayer of the Penitent—Weakness of Faith—Love the fulfilling of the Law—Thankfulness the Life of the Regenerate—My Beloved is Mine and I am His—The Knowledge which is Life Eternal—The Sabbath of Christ found in Meekness—Christ is on the Right Hand of God—The Forgiveness of Sins—Love and Joy in the Spirit—The Warfare and the Armour of Saints—The Love of Christians—The Earthly and Heavenly Citizenship—Mutual Intercessions—Gleanings after Harvest—Bringing unto Christ—Slowness in believing—Grace not given in Vain—The Refiner's Fire—The Lost Crown—Faith in the Incarnation—Value of an Inspired Gospel—The severe and social Virtues—Go and do thou likewise—Joy at hearing the Bridegroom's Voice—The Strength of God in Man's Weakness—Hidden with Christ in God—Do good, hoping for nothing again—The good exchange—War in Heaven—Healing and Peace—The Sacrament of Union—They which shall be accounted Worthy.

and at Oxford and Cambridge

Parochial and Plain Sermons. By JOHN HENRY NEWMAN, B.D., formerly Vicar of St. Mary's, Oxford. Edited by the Rev. W. J. COPELAND, B.D., Rector of Farnham, Essex. New Edition. 8 Vols. Crown 8vo. 5s. each. Sold separately.

CONTENTS OF VOL. I.

Holiness necessary for Future Blessedness—The Immortality of the Soul—Knowledge of God's Will without Obedience—Secret Truths—Self-denial the Test of Religious Earnestness—The Spiritual Mind—Sins of Ignorance and Weakness—God's Commandments not grievous—The Religious use of exalted Feelings—Profession without Practice—Profession without Hypocrisy—Profession without Ostentation—Promising without Doing—Religious Emotion—Religious Faith Rational—The Christian Mysteries—The Self-wise Inquirer—Obedience the Remedy for Religious Perplexity—Times of Private Prayer—Forms of Private Prayer—The Resurrection of the Body—Witnesses of the Resurrection—Christian Reverence—The Religion of the Day—Scripture a Record of Human Sorrow—Christian Manhood.

CONTENTS OF VOL. II.

The World's Benefactors—Faith without Sight—The Incarnation—Martyrdom—Love of Relations and Friends—The Mind of Little Children—Ceremonies of the Church—The Glory of the Christian Church—His Conversion viewed in Reference to His Office—Secrecy and Suddenness of Divine Visitations—Divine Decrees—The Reverence due to Her—Christ, a Quickening Spirit—Saving Knowledge—Self-contemplation—Religious Cowardice—The Gospel Witnesses—Mysteries in Religion—The Indwelling Spirit—The Kingdom of the Saints—The Gospel, a Trust committed to us—Tolerance of Religious Error—Rebuking Sin—The Christian Ministry—Human Responsibility—Guilelessness—The Danger of Riches—The Powers of Nature—The Danger of Accomplishments—Christian Zeal—Use of Saints' Days.

CONTENTS OF VOL. III.

Abraham and Lot—Wilfulness of Israel in rejecting Samuel—Saul—Early years of David—Jeroboam—Faith and Obedience—Christian Repentance—Contracted Views in Religion—A particular Providence as revealed in the Gospel—Tears of Christ at the Grave of Lazarus—Bodily Suffering—The Humiliation of the Eternal Son—Jewish Zeal a Pattern to Christians—Submission to Church Authority—Contest between Truth and Falsehood in the Church—The Church Visible and Invisible—The Visible Church an Encouragement to Faith—The Gift of the Spirit—Regenerating Baptism—Infant Baptism—The Daily Service—The Good Part of Mary—Religious Worship a Remedy for Excitements—Intercession—The Intermediate State.

CONTENTS OF VOL. IV.

The Strictness of the Law of Christ—Obedience without Love, as instanced in the Character of Balaam—Moral Consequences of Single Sins—Acceptance of Religious Privileges compulsory—Reliance on Religious Observances—The Individuality of the Soul—Chastisement amid Mercy—Peace and Joy amid Chastisement—The State of Grace—The Visible Church for the sake of the Elect—The Communion of Saints—The Church a

NEWMAN'S PAROCHIAL AND PLAIN SERMONS—*Continued*.

Home for the Lonely—The Invisible World—The Greatness and Littleness of Human Life—Moral Effects of Communion with God—Christ Hidden from the World—Christ Manifested in Remembrance—The Gainsaying of Korah—The Mysteriousness of our Present Being—The Ventures of Faith—Faith and Love—Watching—Keeping Fast and Festival.

CONTENTS OF VOL. V.

Worship, a Preparation for Christ's Coming—Reverence, a Belief in God's Presence—Unreal Words—Shrinking from Christ's Coming—Equanimity—Remembrance of past Mercies—The Mystery of Godliness—The State of Innocence—Christian Sympathy—Righteousness not of us, but in us—The Law of the Spirit—The New Works of the Gospel—The State of Salvation—Transgressions and Infirmities—Sins of Infirmity—Sincerity and Hypocrisy—The Testimony of Conscience—Many called, few chosen—Present Blessings—Endurance, the Christian's portion—Affliction a School of Comfort—The thought of God, the stay of the Soul—Love the one thing needful—The Power of the Will.

CONTENTS OF VOL. VI.

Fasting, a Source of Trial—Life, the Season of Repentance—Apostolic Abstinence, a Pattern for Christians—Christ's Privations, a Meditation for Christians—Christ the Son of God made Man—The Incarnate Son, a Sufferer and Sacrifice—The Cross of Christ the Measure of the World—Difficulty of realizing Sacred Privileges—The Gospel Sign addressed to Faith—The Spiritual Presence of Christ in the Church—The Eucharistic Presence—Faith the Title for Justification—Judaism of the present day—The Fellowship of the Apostles—Rising with Christ—Warfare the Condition of Victory—Waiting for Christ—Subjection of the Reason and Feelings to the Revealed Word—The Gospel Palaces—The Visible Temple Offerings for the Sanctuary—The Weapons of Saints—Faith without Demonstration—The Mystery of the Holy Trinity—Peace in Believing.

CONTENTS OF VOL. VII.

The Lapse of Time—Religion, a Weariness to the Natural Man—The World our Enemy—The Praise of Men—Temporal Advantages—The Season of Epiphany—The Duty of Self-denial—The Yoke of Christ—Moses the Type of Christ—The Crucifixion—Attendance on Holy Communion—The Gospel Feast—Love of Religion, a new Nature—Religion pleasant to the Religious—Mental Prayer—Infant Baptism—The Unity of the Church—Steadfastness in the Old Paths.

CONTENTS OF VOL. VIII.

Reverence in Worship—Divine Calls—The Trial of Saul—The Call of David—Curiosity a Temptation to Sin—Miracles no remedy for Unbelief—Josiah, a Pattern for the Ignorant—Inward Witness to the Truth of the Gospel—Jeremiah, a Lesson for the Disappointed—Endurance of the World's Censure—Doing Glory to God in Pursuits of the World—Vanity of Human Glory—Truth hidden when not sought after—Obedience to God the Way to Faith in Christ—Sudden Conversions—The Shepherd of our Souls—Religious Joy—Ignorance of Evil.

and at Oxford and Cambridge

NEWMAN'S PAROCHIAL AND PLAIN SERMONS—*Continued.*

"*Dr. Newman's sermons stand by themselves in modern English literature; it might be said, in English literature generally. There have been equally great masterpieces of English writing in this form of composition, and there have been preachers whose theological depth, acquaintance with the heart, earnestness, tenderness, and power have not been inferior to his. But the great writers do not touch, pierce, and get hold of minds as he does, and those who are famous for the power and results of their preaching do not write as he does.*"—SATURDAY REVIEW.

"*They are undeniably models of style in writing of the most faultless kind. As addresses to a miscellaneous multitude they would have been failures; but as addresses to a cultivated audience of university students and tutors they are without a rival.*"—PALL MALL GAZETTE.

"*We have said nothing of the exquisite manner of these sermons, the manner of a mind at once tender and holy, at once loving and austere, at once real and dramatic, at once full of insight into human nature and full of the humility which springs from a higher source.*"—SPECTATOR.

"*We anticipate from the reappearance of the series a large measure of good both to the Church and to individuals; for Dr. Newman's influence as a teacher was, in his Oxford days, almost unrivalled.*"—CHURCH TIMES.

"*In reading these sermons, it is impossible to withhold one's high admiration for the many fine qualities which they display:—plain, unambiguous statement of Christian doctrine according to the preacher's view of it,—practical application of Church dogmas to individual life, character and conduct,—instructive exposition of Scripture, all conveyed in a faultless style and with well-sustained eloquence.*"—NONCONFORMIST.

"*These Sermons may still do much good; and we thank the publishers and editor for the spirit—for it required some—to do this service to religion.*"—CHRISTIAN REMEMBRANCER.

"*Sermon-writers cannot do better than study the clear, sharp, polished, and yet simple style in which the meaning of the once great Anglican preacher is conveyed.*"—ENGLISH CHURCHMAN.

"*The modest and extensive erudition, the large and exact information, the chaste and finished style, and the deep and serious earnestness which combined to give such freshness and force to his spoken discourses, reappear in many of the noble and edifying sermons now before us.*"—WATCHMAN.

"*Few theologians go as deep as Dr. Newman and carry with them the same lucidity of thought and language. In this point, as well as in others, his sermons might well be taken as a model for a pulpit style, even by those who are not always disposed to follow him in his theology.*"— GLASGOW DAILY HERALD.

Lectures on the Doctrine of Justification.
By JOHN HENRY NEWMAN, B.D., sometime Fellow of Oriel College, Oxford. New Edition. Crown 8vo. 5s.

CONTENTS.

Faith considered as the Instrument of Justification—Love considered as the Formal Cause of Justification—Primary Sense of the term Justification—Secondary Senses of the term Justification—Misuse of the term Just or Righteous—On the Gift of Righteousness—The Characteristics of the Gift of Righteousness—Righteousness viewed as a Gift and as a Quality—Righteousness the Fruit of our Lord's Resurrection—The Office of Justifying Faith—The Nature of Justifying Faith—Faith viewed relatively to Rites and Works—On preaching the Gospel—Appendix.

Sermons Bearing upon Subjects of the
DAY. By JOHN HENRY NEWMAN, B.D., sometime Fellow of Oriel College, Oxford. Edited by the Rev. W. J. COPELAND, B.D., Rector of Farnham, Essex. New Edition. Crown 8vo. 5s.

CONTENTS.

The Work of the Christian—Saintliness not forfeited by the Penitent—Our Lord's Last Supper and His First—Dangers to the Penitent—The Three Offices of Christ—Faith and Experience—Faith and the World—The Church and the World—Indulgence in Religious Privileges—Connection between Personal and Public Improvement—Christian Nobleness—Joshua, a Type of Christ and His Followers—Elisha, a Type of Christ and His Followers—The Christian Church a continuation of the Jewish—The Principle of continuity between the Jewish and Christian Churches—The Christian Church an Imperial Power—Sanctity the Token of the Christian Empire—Condition of the Members of the Christian Empire—The Apostolical Christian—Wisdom and Innocence—Invisible Presence of Christ—Outward and Inward Notes of the Church—Grounds for Steadfastness in our Religious Profession—Elijah the Prophet of the Latter Days—Feasting in Captivity—The Parting of Friends.

"*They exhibit all the writer's incisiveness, force of analogy, and wide acquaintance with Scripture.*"—CHURCH REVIEW.
"*Apart from the surpassing literary merits of these discourses, they are memorable as the last words spoken from the pulpit of the English Church by a divine whom all men of all creeds delight to honour.*"—DAILY TELEGRAPH.
"*The pure coinage of a powerful brain, acting under the impulses of an enthusiastic, earnest, and highly conscientious heart.*"—THE ROCK.

Fifteen Sermons preached before the
University of Oxford, between A.D. 1826 and 1843. By JOHN HENRY NEWMAN, B.D., sometime Fellow of Oriel College, Oxford. New Edition. Crown 8vo. 5s.

CONTENTS.

The Philosophical Temper first enjoined by the Gospel—The Influence of Natural and Revealed Religion respectively—Evangelical Sanctity the Perfection of Natural Virtue—The Usurpations of Reason—Personal Influence, the means of Propagating the Truth—Our Justice, as a Principle of Divine Governance—Contest between Faith and Light—Human Responsibility, as Independent of Circumstances—Wilfulness the Sin of Saul—Faith and Reason, contrasted as Habits of Mind—The Nature of Faith in Relation to Reason—Love the Safeguard of Faith against Superstition—Implicit and Explicit Reason—Wisdom, as contrasted with Faith and with Bigotry—The Theory of Developments in Religious Doctrine.

and at Oxford and Cambridge

Sermons Preached on Different Occasions.
By EDWARD MEYRICK GOULBURN, D.D., Dean of Norwich. Fourth Edition. Small 8vo. 6s. 6d.

CONTENTS.

Confession, and the Doctrine of the English Church thereupon—The Moral Instincts which lead Men to the Confessional—Pure Religion and Undefiled—God Keeping and Breaking Silence—The Kingdom that comes not with Observation—Jacob's Dream—The contagious Influence of Faithful Prophesying—Final Impenitence—Final Impenitence exemplified—The Goodness and Severity of God as Manifested in the Atonement—Remedy, the only Form of Doing Good—The Search after Wisdom—The Grounds of True Patriotism—Christ Wielding the Keys of Death and of the World unseen—The Revelation of the Triune God and its Diffusion—The Dispensations—Learning a requisite for the Ministry of the Present Day—Human Instrumentality employed in Man's Salvation—The Stolen Testimony—The Building up of the Family—On Preaching Christ Crucified—Have Salt in Yourselves—The Last Sunday of 1861.

Farewell Counsels of a Pastor to his
Flock, on Topics of the Day. By EDWARD MEYRICK GOULBURN, D.D., Dean of Norwich. Third Edition. Small 8vo. 4s.

CONTENTS.

Absolution—Ritualism—The Doctrine of the Eucharist—The Atonement—The Stability of an Orthodox Faith—The Stability of Personal Religion—On Preaching Christ Crucified—The Responsibility of Hearers.

Warnings of the Holy Week, &c. Being
a Course of Parochial Lectures for the Week before Easter and the Easter Festivals. By the Rev. W. ADAMS, M.A., Author of "Sacred Allegories," &c. Seventh Edition. Small 8vo. 4s. 6d.

CONTENTS.

The Warning given at Bethany—The Warning of the Day of Excitement—The Warning of the Day of Chastisement—The Warning of the Fig Tree—The Warning of Judas—The Warning of Pilate—The Warning of the Day of Rest—The Signs of Our Lord's Presence—The Remedy for Anxious Thoughts—Comfort under Despondency.

Waterloo Place, London

The Catholic Sacrifice. Sermons Preached

at All Saints, Margaret Street. By the Rev. BERDMORE COMPTON, M.A., Vicar of All Saints, Margaret Street. Crown 8vo. 5s.

CONTENTS.

The Eucharistic Life—The Sacrifice of Sweet Savour—The Pure Offering—The Catholic Oblation—The Sacrificial Feast—The Preparation for the Eucharist—The Introductory Office—The Canon—Degrees of Apprehension—The Fascination of Christ Crucified—The Shewbread—Consecration of Worship and Work—Water, Blood, Wine—The Blood of Sprinkling—The Mystery of Sacraments—The Oblation of Gethsemane—Offertory and Tribute Money.

The Sayings of the Great Forty Days,

between the Resurrection and Ascension, regarded as the Outlines of the Kingdom of God. In Five Discourses. With an Examination of Dr. Newman's Theory of Development. By GEORGE MOBERLY, D.C.L., Bishop of Salisbury. Fifth Edition. Crown 8vo. 5s.

Plain Sermons, preached at Brighstone.

By GEORGE MOBERLY, D.C.L., Bishop of Salisbury. Third Edition. Crown 8vo. 5s.

CONTENTS.

Except a Man be Born again—The Lord with the Doctors—The Draw-Net—I will lay me down in Peace—Ye have not so learned Christ—Trinity Sunday—My Flesh is Meat indeed—The Corn of Wheat dying and multiplied—The Seed Corn springing to new Life—I am the Way, the Truth, and the Life—The Ruler of the Sea—Stewards of the Mysteries of God—Ephphatha—The Widow of Nain—Josiah's Discovery of the Law—The Invisible World: Angels—Prayers, especially Daily Prayers—They all with one consent began to make excuse—Ascension Day—The Comforter—The Tokens of the Spirit—Elijah's Warning, Fathers and Children—Thou shalt see them no more for ever—Baskets full of Fragments—Harvest—The Marriage Supper of the Lamb—The Last Judgment.

Sermons preached at Winchester College.

By GEORGE MOBERLY, D.C.L., Bishop of Salisbury. 2 Vols. Small 8vo. 6s. 6d. each. Sold separately.

---

and at Oxford and Cambridge

Sermons. By HENRY MELVILL, B.D., late Canon of St. Paul's, and Chaplain in Ordinary to the Queen. New Edition. 2 Vols. Crown 8vo. 5s. each. Sold separately.

CONTENTS OF VOL. I.

The First Prophecy—Christ the Minister of the Church—The Impossibility of Creature-Merit—The Humiliation of the Man Christ Jesus—The Doctrine of the Resurrection viewed in connection with that of the Soul's Immortality—The Power of Wickedness and Righteousness to reproduce themselves—The Power of Religion to strengthen the Human Intellect—The Provision made by God for the Poor—St. Paul, a Tent-Maker—The Advantages of a state of Expectation—Truth as it is in Jesus—The Difficulties of Scripture.

CONTENTS OF VOL II.

Jacob's Vision and Vow—The continued Agency of the Father and the Son—The Resurrection of Dry Bones—Protestantism and Popery—Christianity a Sword—The Death of Moses—The Ascension of Christ—The Spirit upon the Waters—The Proportion of Grace to Trial—Pleading before the Mountains—Heaven—God's Way in the Sanctuary.

"*Every one who can remember the days when Canon Melvill was the preacher of the day, will be glad to see these four-and-twenty of his sermons so nicely reproduced. His Sermons were all the result of real study and genuine reading, with far more theology in them than those of many who make much more profession of theology. There are sermons here which we can personally remember; it has been a pleasure to us to be reminded of them, and we are glad to see them brought before the present generation. We hope that they may be studied, for they deserve it thoroughly.*"—LITERARY CHURCHMAN.

"*The Sermons of Canon Melvill, now republished in two handy volumes, need only to be mentioned to be sure of a hearty welcome. Sound learning, well-weighed words, calm and keen logic, and solemn devoutness, mark the whole series of masterly discourses, which embrace some of the chief doctrines of the Church, and set them forth in clear and Scriptural strength.*"—STANDARD.

"*It would be easy to quote portions of exceeding beauty and power. It was not, however, the charm of style, nor wealth of words, both which Canon Melvill possessed in so great abundance, that he relied on to win souls; but the power and spirit of Him Who said, 'I, if I be lifted up, will draw all men to Me.'*"—RECORD.

"*Messrs. Rivington have published very opportunely, at a time when Churchmen are thinking with satisfaction of the new blood infused into the Chapter of St. Paul's, Sermons by Henry Melvill, who in his day was as celebrated as a preacher as is Canon Liddon now. The sermons are not only couched in elegant language, but are replete with matter which the younger clergy would do well to study.*"—JOHN BULL.

"*Few preachers have had more admirers than the Rev. Henry Melvill, and the new edition of his Sermons, in two volumes, will doubtless find plenty of purchasers. The Sermons abound in thought, and the thoughts are couched in English which is at once elegant in construction and easy to read.*"—CHURCH TIMES.

". . . . "*As they are models of their particular style of oratory, they will be valuable helps to young preachers.*"—UNION REVIEW.

"*Henry Melvill's intellect was large, his imagination brilliant, his ardour intense, and his style strong, fervid, and picturesque. Often he seemed to glow with the inspiration of a prophet.*"—AMERICAN QUARTERLY CHURCH REVIEW.

Sermons on Certain of the Less

Prominent Facts and References in Sacred Story. By HENRY MELVILL, B.D., late Canon of St. Paul's, and Chaplain in Ordinary to the Queen. New Edition. 2 Vols. Crown 8vo. 5s. each. Sold separately.

CONTENTS OF VOL. I.

The Faith of Joseph on his Death-bed—Angels as Remembrancers—The Burning of the Magical Books—The Parting Hymn—Cæsar's Household—The Sleepless Night—The Well of Bethlehem—The Thirst of Christ—The second Delivery of the Lord's Prayer—Peculiarities in the Miracle in the Coasts of Decapolis—The Latter Rain—The Lowly Errand—Nehemiah before Artaxerxes—Jabez.

CONTENTS OF VOL. II.

The Young Man in the Linen Cloth—The Fire on the Shore—The Finding the Guest-Chamber—The Spectre's Sermon a truism—Various Opinions—The Misrepresentations of Eve—Seeking, after Finding—The Bird's Nest—Angels our Guardians in trifles—The appearance of failure—Simon the Cyrenian—The power of the Eye—Pilate's Wife—The Examination of Cain.

" We are glad to see this new edition of what we have always considered to be Melvill's best sermons, because in them we have his best thoughts. . . . Many of these sermons are the strongest arguments yet adduced for internal evidence of the veracity of the Scriptural narratives."—STANDARD.

" Polished, classical, and winning, these sermons bear the marks of literary labour. A study of them will aid the modern preacher to refine and polish his discourses, and to add to the vigour which is now the fashion, the graces of chastened eloquence and winning rhetoric."—ENGLISH CHURCHMAN.

" The sermons of the lamented Melvill are too well known to require any commendation from us. We have here all the power of rhetoric, and the grace and beauty of style, for which the author has been distinguished, and which have contributed to render him a model to preachers, and given him a representative position in the history of the English pulpit."—WEEKLY REVIEW.

' Unusually interesting . . . . No one can read these sermons without deriving instruction from them, without being compelled to acknowledge that new light has been cast for him on numerous passages of Scripture, which he must henceforth read with greater intelligence and greater interest than before." — EDINBURGH COURANT.

" For skill in developing the significance of the ' less prominent facts of Holy Scripture' no one could compete with the late Canon Melvill, four volumes of whose discourses—two of them occupied entirely with his sermons on subjects of this class—are before us. His preaching was unique. He selected for the most part texts that are not frequently treated, and when he chose those of a more ordinary character, he generally presented them in new light, and elicited from them some truth which would not have suggested itself to any other preacher. He was singularly ingenious in some of his conceptions, and wonderfully forcible and impressive in his mode of developing and applying them."—NONCONFORMIST.

" The publishers of these well-known, almost classic sermons, have conferred a boon on all lovers of our pulpit literature by this beautiful, portable edition of some of the most brilliant and original discourses that have been delivered to this generation."—BRITISH QUARTERLY REVIEW.

Selection from the Sermons preached

during the Latter Years of his Life, in the Parish Church of Barnes, and in the Cathedral of St. Paul's. By HENRY MELVILL, B.D., late Canon of St. Paul's, and Chaplain in Ordinary to the Queen. New Edition. 2 Vols. Crown 8vo. 5s. each. Sold separately.

CONTENTS OF VOL. I.

The Parity of the consequences of Adam's Transgression and Christ's Death—The Song of Simeon—The Days of Old—Omissions of Scripture—The Madman in Sport—Peace, Peace, when there is no Peace—A very ovely Song—This is that King Ahaz—Ariel—New Wine and Old Bottles—Demas—Michael and the Devil—The Folly of Excessive Labour—St. Paul at Philippi—Believing a Lie—The Prodigal Son—The Foolishness of Preaching—Knowledge and Sorrow—The Unjust Steward—The Man born blind.

CONTENTS OF VOL. II.

Rejoicing as in Spoil — Satan a Copyist — The binding the Tares nto Bundles — Two walking together—Agreeing with the Adversary—God speaking to Moses—Hoping in Mercy—Faith as a Grain of Mustard Seed—Mary's Recompense—War in Heaven—Glory into Shame—The Last Judgment—Man like to Vanity—God so Loved the World—Saul—And what shall this Man do?—The Sickness and Death of Elisha—Abiding in our Callings—Trinity Sunday.

"*The main characteristics of Canon Melvill's sermons are these—they are not polemical; the* odium theologicum *is nowhere to be found in them, and nowhere is the spirit of true Christian charity and love absent from them. This will widen their usefulness, for they will on this account make a ready way amongst all sects and creeds of professing Christians. Again, these sermons are eminently practical and devotional in their tone and aim. The truths here proclaimed pierce the heart to its very core, so true is the preacher's aim, so vigorous is the force with which he shoots the convictions of his own heart into the hearts of his hearers.*"—STANDARD.

"*There are in the sermons before us all Melvill's wonted grace of diction, strength of reasoning, and aptness of illustration.*"—WEEKLY REVIEW.

"*Two other volumes of the late Canon Melvill's sermons contain forty discourses preached by him in his later years, and they are prefaced by a short memoir of one of the worthiest and most impressive preachers of recent times.*"—EXAMINER.

"*Many years have now elapsed since we first heard Henry Melvill. But we can still recall the text, the sermon, the deep impression made upon us by the impassioned eloquence of the great preacher. It was our first, and very profitable experience of what influence there resides in the faithful preaching of the Gospel of the Lord Jesus Christ. For while it was impossible to be indifferent to the messenger, yet the message was brought home by him to the heart and to the conscience. It is pleasant in these, the latest sermons delivered by Mr. Melvill, to find the same faithful utterance.*"—CHRISTIAN OBSERVER.

Lectures delivered at St. Margaret's,

Lothbury. By the Rev. HENRY MELVILL, B.D., late Canon of St. Paul's, and Chaplain in Ordinary to the Queen. New Edition. Crown 8vo. 5s.

CONTENTS.

The Return of the Dispossessed Spirit—Honey from the Rock—Easter—The Witness in Oneself—The Apocrypha—A Man a Hiding-place—The Hundredfold Recompense—The Life more than Meat—Isaiah's Vision—St. John the Baptist—Building the Tombs of the Prophets—Manifestation of the Sons of God—St. Paul's Determination—The Song of Moses and the Lamb—The Divine Longsuffering—Sowing the Seed—The Great Multitude—The Kinsman Redeemer—St. Barnabas—Spiritual Decline.

Sermons on Special Occasions.

By DANIEL MOORE, M.A., Chaplain in Ordinary to the Queen, and Vicar of Holy Trinity, Paddington. Crown 8vo. 7s. 6d.

CONTENTS.

The Words of Christ imperishable—The Gospel Welcome—The Conversion of St. Paul—The Christian's Mission—Business and Godliness—Soberness and Watchfulness—The Joy of the Disciples at the Resurrection—The Saviour's Ascension—Jesus in the Midst—The Moral Attractions of the Cross—The Gospel Workmen—The Work of the Holy Spirit—The Doctrine of the Holy Trinity—The Law of Moral Recompenses—The Goodness of King Joash—The Tenderness of Christ—Christ our Example in Youth—Jacob in Life and in Death—The Spiritual Mind—Britain's Obligations to the Gospel—The Throne in Mourning—Prayer and Providence—The Unsearchableness of God.

The Age and the Gospel;

Four Sermons preached before the University of Cambridge, at the Hulsean Lecture, 1864. With a Discourse on Final Retribution. By DANIEL MOORE, M.A., Chaplain in Ordinary to the Queen, and Vicar of Holy Trinity, Paddington. Crown 8vo. 5s.

and at Oxford and Cambridge

Sermons preached before the University of Oxford, and on various occasions. By J. B. MOZLEY, D.D., Regius Professor of Divinity, Oxford, and Canon of Christ Church. 8vo. 10s. 6d.

CONTENTS.

The Roman Council—The Pharisees—Eternal Life—The Reversal of Human Judgment—War—Nature—The Work of the Spirit on the Natural Man—The Atonement—Our Duty to Equals—The Peaceful Temper—The Strength of Wishes—The unspoken Judgment of Mankind—The true test of Spiritual Birth—Ascension Day—Gratitude—The Principle of Emulation—Religion the First Choice—The Influence of Dogmatic Teaching on Education.

The Mystery of the Temptation: a Course of Lectures. By the Rev. W. H. HUTCHINGS, M.A., Sub-Warden of the House of Mercy, Clewer. Crown 8vo. 4s. 6d.

CONTENTS.

The Entrance into the Temptation—The Fast—The Personality of Satan—The First Temptation—The Second Temptation—The Third Temptation—The End of the Temptation.

"*We can mention with unmixed praise a series of lectures on ‘The Mystery of the Temptation,' by Mr. Hutchings of Clewer. They are deeply thoughtful, full, and well-written, in a style which, from its calmness and dignity, befits the subject.*"—GUARDIAN.

"*This book is one of the refreshing proofs still occasionally met with that the traditional culture and refinement of the Anglican clergy is not quite exhausted, nor its exhaustion implied, by the endless and vulgar controversies that fill the columns of religious newspapers. The sober earnestness that has always been a characteristically Anglican virtue has not failed in a preacher like Mr. Hutchings.*"—ACADEMY.

"*Students of Scripture will find in ‘The Mystery of the Temptation' sound reasoning, the evidences of close study, and the spirit of reverence and fervent faith.*"—MORNING POST.

"*This is a volume of lectures which will repay serious study. They are earnest to the last degree.*"—LITERARY CHURCHMAN.

"*Very good indeed.*"—NEW YORK CHURCH JOURNAL.

The Soul in its Probation: Sermons Preached at the Church of S. Alban the Martyr, Holborn, on the Sundays in Lent, 1873. By the Rev. F. N. OXENHAM, M.A. 8vo. 5s.

The Religion of the Christ: its Historic and Literary Development considered as an Evidence of its Origin. Being the Bampton Lectures for 1874. By the Rev. STANLEY LEATHES, M.A., Minister of St. Philip's, Regent Street, and Professor of Hebrew, King's College, London. Second Edition. Crown 8vo. 7s. 6d.

"*These lectures are a noble contribution to the evidences of the Christian faith.*"—BRITISH QUARTERLY REVIEW.

"*Admirably adapted to meet some of the foremost objections which are now being brought against 'the divine authority of the Holy Scriptures.' We earnestly recommend our readers to buy the book for themselves.*"—LITERARY CHURCHMAN.

"*A volume which ought to take its place beside the best standard works on the evidences of Christianity—a kind of literature in which the Church of England is peculiarly rich.*"—SCOTSMAN.

"*His Bampton Lectures are perhaps the most suggestive and elaborate of all his productions, and would of themselves win for him a high position as a writer on Christian evidence.*"—FREEMAN.

"*The preface, in which Mr. Leathes sums up the arguments in his lucid way, which are more elaborately drawn out in the Lectures, is one of the finest specimens of clear, candid, temperate reasoning in modern literature.*"—NEW YORK INDEPENDENT.

"*With thoughtful minds it will carry great weight.*"—NEW YORK CHURCHMAN.

The Witness of the Old Testament to Christ. Being the Boyle Lectures for the year 1868. By the Rev. STANLEY LEATHES, M.A., Minister of St. Philip's, Regent Street, and Professor of Hebrew, King's College, London. 8vo. 9s.

The Witness of St. Paul to Christ. Being the Boyle Lectures for 1869. With an Appendix on the Credibility of the Acts, in Reply to the Recent Strictures of Dr. Davidson. By the Rev. STANLEY LEATHES, M.A., Minister of St. Philip's, Regent Street, and Professor of Hebrew, King's College, London. 8vo. 10s. 6d.

The Witness of St. John to Christ. Being the Boyle Lectures for 1870. With an Appendix on the Authorship and Integrity of St. John's Gospel, and the Unity of the Johannine Writings. By the Rev. STANLEY LEATHES, M.A., Minister of St. Philip's, Regent Street, and Professor of Hebrew, King's College, London. 8vo. 10s. 6d.

and at Oxford and Cambridge

The Permanence of Christianity. Con-
sidered in Eight Lectures preached before the University of
Oxford, in the year 1872, on the Foundation of the late Rev.
John Bampton, M.A. By JOHN RICHARD TURNER EATON,
M.A., late Fellow and Tutor of Merton College, Rector of
Lapworth, Warwickshire. 8vo. 12s.

Short Sermons on the Psalms in their
Order. Preached in a Village Church. By W. J. STRACEY,
M.A., Rector of Oxnead, and Vicar of Buxton, Norfolk, for-
merly Fellow of Magdalen College, Cambridge. Crown 8vo.

    Vol. I.—Psalms I—XXV. 5s.
    Vol. II.—Psalms XXVI—LI. 5s.

Twelve Addresses at his Visitation
of the Cathedral and Diocese of Lincoln, in the year
MDCCCLXXIII. By CHR. WORDSWORTH, D.D., Bishop of
Lincoln. Crown 8vo. 3s. 6d.

The Church of England and the
Maccabees; or, The History of the Maccabees considered
with reference to the Present Condition and Prospects of the
Church. Two Sermons. By CHR. WORDSWORTH, D.D.,
Bishop of Lincoln. Second Edition. Small 8vo. 1s.

The Home Life of Jesus of Nazareth,
and other Sermons. By the Rev. AUGUSTUS GURNEY, M.A.,
Vicar of Wribbenhall, Kidderminster. Crown 8vo. 5s.

The Perfect Man ; or, Jesus an Example
of Godly Life. By the Rev. HARRY JONES, M.A., Rector of S. George-in-the-East. Second Edition. Crown 8vo. 3s. 6d.

Life in the World; being a Selection
from Sermons preached at S. Luke's, Berwick Street. By the Rev. HARRY JONES, M.A., Rector of S. George-in-the-East. Second Edition. Crown 8vo. 5s.

Sermons on Various Subjects. By the
Rev. W. J. HALL, M.A., Rector of S. Clement's Eastcheap with S. Martin's Orgar, and Minor Canon of S. Paul's Cathedral. Crown 8vo. 5s.

Sermons Preached in a Country Village.
By the Rev. T. K. ARNOLD, M.A., late Rector of Lyndon. Post 8vo. 5s. 6d.

Six Short Sermons on Sin. Lent Lectures
at S. Alban the Martyr, Holborn. By the Rev. ORBY SHIPLEY, M.A. Fifth Edition. Small 8vo. 1s.

The Way of Holiness in Married Life.
A Course of Sermons preached in Lent. By the Rev. HENRY J. ELLISON, M.A., Hon. Canon of Christ Church, and Vicar of New Windsor, Berks. Second Edition. Small 8vo. 2s. 6d.

Parochial Sermons preached in a Village
Church. Fourth Series. By the Rev. CHARLES A. HEURTLEY, D.D., Margaret Professor of Divinity, and Canon of Christ Church, Oxford. Crown 8vo. 5s. 6d.

---

and at Oxford and Cambridge

The Last Three Sermons preached at

Oxford by PHILIP N. SHUTTLEWORTH, D.D., sometime Lord Bishop of Chichester. Justification through Faith—The Merciful Character of the Gospel Covenant—The Sufficiency of Scripture a Rule of Faith. To which is added a Letter addressed in 1841 to a Young Clergyman, now a Priest in the Church of Rome. New Edition. Small 8vo. 2s. 6d.

The Christian Character; Six Sermons

preached in Lent. By JOHN JACKSON, D.D., Bishop of London. Seventh Edition. Small 8vo. 3s. 6d.

Simple Sermons. By the Rev. W. H.

RANKEN, M.A., Fellow of Corpus Christi College, Oxford, and Rector of Meysey Hampton, near Cricklade. Small 8vo. 5s.

Faith and Practice: A Selection of

Sermons Preached in St. Philip's Chapel, Regent Street. By the Rev. FRANCIS PIGOU, M.A., Vicar of Halifax, and Hon. Chaplain in Ordinary to the Queen. Small 8vo. 6s.

CONTENTS.

The Certainty of the Resurrection—Whitsunday—The Stilling of the Tempest—Practical Religion—The Memory of the Just—The Remembrance of Sin—The Danger of Relapse—Individual Influence—The use and abuse of God's gifts—Natural and Spiritual Instincts—Prayer—Preparation for Death.

7. Religious Education.

A Key to Christian Doctrine and Practice,

founded on the Church Catechism. By the Rev. JOHN HENRY BLUNT, M.A., F.S.A., Editor of "The Annotated Book of Common Prayer," &c. &c. Small 8vo. 2s. 6d.

Forming a Volume of "Keys to Christian Knowledge."

"Of cheap and reliable text-books of this nature there has hitherto been a great want. We are often asked to recommend books for use in Church Sunday-schools, and we therefore take this opportunity of saying that we know of none more likely to be of service both to teachers and scholars than these 'Keys.'" — CHURCHMAN'S SHILLING MAGAZINE.

"This is another of Mr. Blunt's most useful manuals, with all the precision of a school book, yet diverging into matters of practical application so freely as to make it most serviceable, either as a teacher's suggestion book, or as an intelligent pupil's reading book." — LITERARY CHURCHMAN.

" Will be very useful for the higher classes in Sunday-schools, or rather for the fuller instruction of the Sunday-school teachers themselves, where the parish priest is wise enough to devote a certain time regularly to their preparation for their voluntary task." — UNION REVIEW.

Household Theology: a Handbook of

Religious Information respecting the Holy Bible, the Prayer Book, the Church, the Ministry, Divine Worship, the Creeds, &c. &c. By the Rev. JOHN HENRY BLUNT, M.A., F.S.A., Editor of "The Annotated Book of Common Prayer," &c. &c. New Edition. Small 8vo. 3s. 6d.

CONTENTS.

The Bible—The Prayer Book—The Church—Table of Dates—Ministerial Offices—Divine Worship—The Creeds—A Practical Summary of Christian Doctrine—The Great Christian Writers of Early Times—Ancient and Modern Heresies and Sects—The Church Calendar—A short explanation of Words used in Church History and Theology—Index.

Manuals of Religious Instruction.

Edited by JOHN PILKINGTON NORRIS, B.D., Canon of Bristol, and Examining Chaplain to the Bishop of Manchester.

3 Volumes. Small 8vo. 3s. 6d. each. Sold separately.

The Old Testament.
The New Testament.
The Prayer Book.

Or each Volume in Five Parts. 1s. each Part.

[These Manuals are intended to supply a five years' course of instruction for young people between the ages of thirteen and eighteen.

It will be seen that fifteen small graduated text-books are provided :—

Five on the Old Testament ;
Five on the New Testament ;
Five on the Catechism and Liturgy.

In preparing the last, the Editor has thought it best to spread the study of the Catechism over several years, rather than compress it into one.

This may give rise to what may appear some needless repetition. But the Lessons of our Catechism are of such paramount importance, that it seems desirable to keep it continually in our Pupils' hands, as the best key to the study of the Prayer Book.

There has been a grievous want of *definiteness* in our young people's knowledge of Church doctrine. Especially have the Diocesan Inspectors noticed it in our Pupil Teachers. It has arisen, doubtless, from their Teachers assuming that they had clear elementary ideas about religion, in which really they had never been grounded. It is therefore thought not too much to ask them to give one-third of their time to the study of the Prayer Book.

In the Old Testament and New Testament Manuals the greatest pains have been taken to give them such a character as shall render it impossible for them to supersede the Sacred Text. Two main objects the writers of the Old and New Testament Manuals have proposed to themselves; first, to stimulate interest; second, to supply a sort of running commentary on the inspired page. Especial pains have been taken to draw the reader's attention to the *spiritual* teaching of Holy Scripture, and to subordinate to this the merely historical interest.

The writer of the Old Testament Manual has made it his endeavour to help the reader to see our Lord Christ in Law, in Psalms, in Prophets.

The New Testament Manual is confined to the Gospels and Acts. It was found impossible to include any of the Epistles. But the Fourth Part of the Prayer Book Manual will in some measure supply this deficiency.

Although they were originally prepared with special regard to Pupil Teachers, they willll be found adapted also for all students of a like age (from thirteen to eighteen) who have not access to many books.]

Waterloo Place, London

Rudiments of Theology. A First Book

for Students. By JOHN PILKINGTON NORRIS, B.D., Canon of Bristol, and Examining Chaplain to the Bishop of Manchester. Crown 8vo. 7s. 6d.

"*It is altogether a remarkable book. We have seldom seen clear, incisive reasoning, orthodox teaching, and wide-mindedness in such happy combination.*"—LITERARY CHURCHMAN.

"*A most useful book for theological students in the earlier part of their course. . . . The book is one for which the Church owes a debt of gratitude to Canon Norris, combining, as it does, orthodoxy and learning, and logical accuracy of definition with real charity. We heartily commend it.*"—JOHN BULL.

"*We can recommend this book to theological students as a useful and compendious manual. It is clear and well arranged. . . . We venture to believe that, on the whole, he is a very fair exponent of the teaching of the English Church, and that his book may be profitably used by those for whom it is chiefly intended—that is, candidates for ordination.*"—SPECTATOR.

"*This is a work of real help to candidates for ordination and to the general student of theology.*"—STANDARD.

"*An admirable theological text-book, that cannot fail to be acceptable to all Churchmen desirous of an insight into the principles of theology, as well as to that class—candidates for ordination—for whom it was specially designed.*"—SCOTTISH GUARDIAN.

"*This work was prepared as a hand-book for theological students. But it is to reach a far wider field. It is capable of doing a most important service among all classes. We have seldom, if ever, met a more satisfactory or a clearer presentation of the fundamental facts of theology than those given in these pages. . . . The author has the rare faculty—it amounts really to genius—of saying just the thing that ought to be said, and of presenting any truth in such a shape that the reader can easily take hold of it and make it his own. . . . We commend this work to Churchmen generally as one from which all can derive profit. To the Clergy it will serve as a model method of dogmatic teaching, and to the laity it will be a rich storehouse of information concerning the things to be believed. . . . The whole thing is so admirable in tone, arrangement, and style that it will, no doubt, become universally popular.*"—CHURCHMAN (NEW YORK).

The Young Churchman's Companion

to the Prayer Book. By the Rev. J. W. GEDGE, M.A., Diocesan Inspector of Schools for the Archdeaconry of Surrey. (Recommended by the late and present Lord Bishops of Winchester.)

Part I.—Morning and Evening Prayer and Litany.
Part II.—Baptismal and Confirmation Services.

18mo., 1s. each Part; or in paper cover, 6d.

𝖆𝖓𝖉 𝖆𝖙 𝕺𝖝𝖋𝖔𝖗𝖉 𝖆𝖓𝖉 𝕮𝖆𝖒𝖇𝖗𝖎𝖉𝖌𝖊

Catechesis: or, Christian Instruction

preparatory to Confirmation and First Communion. By CHARLES WORDSWORTH, D.C.L., Bishop of St. Andrews. New Edition. Small 8vo. 2s.

A Help to Catechizing. For the Use of

Clergymen, Schools, and Private Families. By JAMES BEAVEN, D.D., formerly Professor of Divinity in the University of King's College, Toronto. New Edition. 18mo. 1s.

Catechetical Exercises on the Apostles'

Creed; chiefly from Bp. Pearson. By EDWARD BICKERSTETH, D.D., Dean of Lichfield. New Edition. 18mo. 2s.

Questions Illustrating the Thirty-nine

Articles. By EDWARD BICKERSTETH, D.D., Dean of Lichfield. Fifth Edition. 12mo. 3s. 6d.

A Glossary of Ecclesiastical Terms.

Containing Brief Explanations of Words used in Theology, Liturgiology, Chronology, Law, Architecture, Antiquities, Symbolism, Greek Hierology and Mediæval Latin; together with some account of Titles of our Lord, Emblems of Saints, Hymns, Orders, Heresies, Ornaments, Offices, Vestments and Ceremonial, and Miscellaneous Subjects. By Various Writers. Edited by the Rev. ORBY SHIPLEY, M.A. Crown 8vo. 18s.

Plain Sermons on the Latter Part of

the Catechism: being the Conclusion of the Series contained in the Ninth Volume of "Plain Sermons." By the Rev. ISAAC WILLIAMS, B.D., formerly Fellow of Trinity College, Oxford, Author of "A Devotional Commentary on the Gospel Narrative," &c. 8vo. 6s. 6d.

Waterloo Place, London

The Idle Word: Short Religious Essays upon the Gift of Speech. By EDWARD MEYRICK GOULBURN, D.D., Dean of Norwich. Fourth Edition. Small 8vo.

CONTENTS

The Connexion of Speech with Reason—The Connexion of Speech with Reason—The Heavenly Analogy of the Connexion of Speech with Reason—An Idle Word Defined from the Decalogue—An Idle Word defined from the Decalogue—What is an Idle Word?—Words of Blessing and Innocent Pleasantry not Idle—Speech the Instrument of Progress and Sacrifice—Hints for the Guidance of Conversation—On Religious Conversation—Appendix.

A Manual of Confirmation, Comprising—1. A General Account of the Ordinance. 2. The Baptismal Vow, and the English Order of Confirmation, with Short Notes, Critical and Devotional. 3. Meditations and Prayers on Passages of Holy Scripture, in connexion with the Ordinance. With a Pastoral Letter instructing Catechumens how to prepare themselves for their first Communion. By EDWARD MEYRICK GOULBURN, D.D., Dean of Norwich. Ninth Edition. Small 8vo.

8. Allegories and Tales.

Allegories and Tales. By the Rev. W. E. HEYGATE, M.A., Rector of Brighstone. Crown 8vo. 5s.

"*It is eminently original, and every one of its sixty-three short allegories is a story that the dullest child will read and the intelligent child will understand and enjoy. Grave thought, kindly raillery, biting sarcasm, grim humour, sincere indignation, wise counsel, a broad charity, and other characteristics, run through the allegories, many of which are highly poetical and good models of that style of composition.*"—EDINBURGH COURANT.

"*Mr. Heygate's volume contains about sixty short tales or allegories, all rife with good teaching, plainly set forth, and written in a very engaging and attractive style. As a present for children this book would be at once acceptable and beneficial. It can be highly commended.*"—CHURCH HERALD.

"*There are both grace and precision about these 'Allegories and Tales,' which make them charming to read either for young or for old. The stories are some of them quaint, some of them picturesque, all of them pleasant; and the moral they inclose shines out soft and clear as through a crystal. This is a book that may be recommended for a present, not only for young people, but for those of larger growth.*"—ATHENÆUM.

"*The Rector of Brighstone has the gift of writing moral and spiritual lessons for the young in the most attractive fashion. His 'Allegories and Tales' are excellent specimens of stories, with a moral, in which the moral is not obtrusive and yet is not lost.*"—ENGLISH INDEPENDENT.

"*A book of very great beauty and power. Mr. Heygate is a thoughtful, earnest and able writer, on whom more than any one is fallen in a striking manner the mantle of the great author of 'Agathos.'*"—JOHN BULL.

Soimême; a Story of a Wilful Life. Small 8vo. 3s. 6d.

"*There is a very quiet, earnest tone in this story, which reconciles the reader to the lesson which it is intended to teach. It is essentially a story of character, and the heroine who is supposed to relate it is presented in a clearly defined and somewhat picturesque manner . . . To the thoughtful who are passing from youth to riper years, 'Soimême' will prove both attractive and useful.*"—PUBLIC OPINION.

"*A vein of lofty, moral, and deep religious feeling runs through the whole tale, and the author neither proses nor preaches.*"—STANDARD.

"*A very natural, unaffected, and simple little story for young people—one which they will not only read but enjoy.*"—MORNING HERALD.

"*The author promises to become a valuable accession to the ranks of our popular lady writers. 'Soimême' is a simple life-like story, charmingly told and gracefully written, and, what is better still, its tendencies are excellent. The lessons it teaches are of the highest order.*"—EUROPEAN MAIL.

"*There are many clever little bits of description, and excellent maxims worth remembering. The scenery is all charmingly described.*"—MONTHLY PACKET.

Waterloo Place, London

The First Chronicle of Æscendune.

A Tale of the Days of Saint Dunstan. By the Rev. A. D. CRAKE, B.A., Chaplain of All Saints' School, Bloxham, Author of the "History of the Church under the Roman Empire," &c. &c. Crown 8vo. 3s. 6d.

"*The volume will possess a strong interest, especially for the young, and be useful, too, for though in form a tale, it may be classed among 'the side-lights of history.'*"—STANDARD.

"*Altogether the book shows great thought and careful study of the manners and customs of those early Saxon times.*"—JOHN BULL.

"*We shall be glad when Mr. Crake takes up his pen once more, to give us a further instalment of the annals of the House of Æscendune.*"—CHURCH TIMES.

"*A very interesting and well written story of Saxon times—the times of Dunstan and the hapless Edwy. The author has evidently taken great pains to examine into the real history of the period. We can scarcely imagine it possible that it should be anything else than a great favourite.*"—LITERARY CHURCHMAN.

"*It is one of the best historical tales for the young that has been published for a long time.*"—NONCONFORMIST.

"*Written with much spirit and a careful attention to the best authorities on the history of the period of which he treats.*"—NATIONAL CHURCH.

"*The facts upon which the Chronicle is based have been carefully brought together from a variety of sources, and great skill has been shown in the construction of the narrative. The aim of the author is certainly a good one, and his efforts have been attended with a considerable amount of success.*"—ROCK.

Alfgar the Dane, or the Second Chronicle of Æscendune.

A Tale. By the Rev. A. D. CRAKE, B.A., Chaplain of All Saints' School, Bloxham, Author of the "History of the Church under the Roman Empire," &c. &c. Crown 8vo. 3s. 6d.

"*Mr. Crake's 'Chronicles of Æscendune' have their second instalment in 'Alfgar the Dane,' a youth who is saved from the massacre on S. Brice's night to meet with many capital adventures.*"—GUARDIAN.

"*Sure to be excessively popular with boys, and we look forward with great interest to the Third Chronicle, which will tell of the Norman invasion.*"—CHURCH TIMES.

"*As in his former production, Mr. Crake seems to have taken great pains to be correct in his facts, and he has, we really believe, combined accuracy with liveliness. Schoolboys, not at Bloxham only, ought to be very grateful to him; though in thus speaking we by no means intend to imply that seniors will not find this little book both interesting and instructive. Its tone is as excellent as that of Mr. Crake's previous tale.*"—CHURCH QUARTERLY REVIEW.

"*Here, strung together with characters in harmony with the times, is a thoroughly well written history of the later Danish invasions of England. . . . . As a tale his work is interesting; as a history it is of very considerable value.*"—NONCONFORMIST.

"*It is not often that a writer combines so completely the qualities which go to make up the historian and the novelist, but Mr. Crake has this happy conjunction of faculties in an eminent degree.*"—STANDARD.

and at Oxford and Cambridge

The Hillford Confirmation. A Tale.
By M. C. PHILLPOTTS. New Edition. 16mo. 1s.

Sacred Allegories. The Shadow of the
Cross—The Distant Hills—The Old Man's Home—The King's Messengers. By the Rev. WILLIAM ADAMS, M.A., late Fellow of Merton College, Oxford. New Edition. With numerous Illustrations. Small 8vo. 5s.

The Four Allegories may be had separately, with Illustrations. Small 8vo. 1s. each.

Herbert Tresham; a Tale of the Great
Rebellion. By the Rev. JOHN MASON NEALE, D.D., late Warden of Sackville College, East Grinsted. New Edition. Small 8vo. 3s. 6d.

Semele; or, The Spirit of Beauty: a
Venetian Tale. By the Rev. J. D. MEREWEATHER, B.A. English Chaplain at Venice. Small 8vo. 3s. 6d.

9. History and Biography.

A Christian Painter of the Nineteenth
Century; being the Life of Hippolyte Flandrin. By the Author of "A Dominican Artist," "Life of S. Francis de Sales," &c. Crown 8vo. 7s. 6d.

"This is a touching and instructive story of a life singularly full of nobility, affection, and grace, and it is worthily told."—SPECTATOR.

"Sympathetic, popular, and free, almost to a fault, from technicalities. . . . The book is welcome as a not untimely memorial to a man who deserves to be held up as an example."—SATURDAY REVIEW.

"This is a charming addition to biographical literature."—NOTES AND QUERIES.

"L'auteur anglais a traduit, avec une profonde connaissance des deux langues, ces lettres intimes du grand artiste que nous connaissions déjà, et a complété sa biographie par des détails nouveaux et curieux sur les années qu'il a passées à Rome."—GAZETTE DES BEAUX-ARTS (PARIS).

"The record of a life marked by exalted aims, and crowned by no small amount of honour and success, cannot but be welcome to earnest students of all kinds. . . . There are many fine pieces of criticism in this book,—utterances of Flandrin's which show the clear wit of the man, his candour, and self-balanced judgment. . . . We have written enough to show how interesting the book is."—ATHENÆUM.

"The letters have the rare charm of being delightfully translated."—GUARDIAN.

"We have not seen, in many years, a book of biography more fascinating than this."—NEW YORK CHURCHMAN.

Bossuet and his Contemporaries. By
the Author of "Life of S. Francis de Sales," "A Dominican Artist," &c. Crown 8vo. 12s.

"It contains so many interesting facts that it may be profitably read even by those who already know the man and the period."—SPECTATOR.

"Here is a clear and good work, the product of thorough industry and of honest mind."—NONCONFORMIST.

"All biography is delightful, and this story of Bossuet is eminently so."—NOTES AND QUERIES.

"Bossuet's daily life, his style of preaching, his association with the stirring political, social, and ecclesiastical events of his time, are presented in a simple but picturesque way."—DAILY NEWS.

"We are always glad to welcome a fresh work from the graceful pen of the author of 'A Dominican Artist.'"—SATURDAY REVIEW.

---

and at Oxford and Cambridge

A Dominican Artist: A Sketch of the

Life of the Rev. Père Besson, of the Order of St. Dominic. By the Author of "The Life of Madame Louise de France," &c. New Edition. Crown 8vo. 6s.

"*The author of the Life of Père Besson writes with a grace and refinement of devotional feeling peculiarly suited to a subject-matter which suffers beyond most others from any coarseness of touch. It would be difficult to find 'the simplicity and purity of a holy life' more exquisitely illustrated than in Father Besson's career, both before and after his joining the Dominican Order under the auspices of Lacordaire. . . . Certainly we have never come across what could more strictly be termed in the truest sense 'the life of a beautiful soul.' The author has done well in presenting to English readers this singularly graceful biography, in which all who can appreciate genuine simplicity and nobleness of Christian character will find much to admire and little or nothing to condemn.*"—SATURDAY REVIEW.

"*It would indeed have been a deplorable omission had so exquisite a biography been by any neglect lost to English readers, and had a character so perfect in its simple and complete devotion been withheld from our admiration. . . . . But we have dwelt too long already on this fascinating book, and must now leave it to our readers.*"—LITERARY CHURCHMAN.

"*A beautiful and most interesting sketch of the late Père Besson, an artist who forsook the easel for the altar.*"—CHURCH TIMES.

"*Whatever a reader may think of Père Besson's profession as a monk, no one will doubt his goodness; no one can fail to profit who will patiently read his life, as here written by a friend, whose sole defect is in being slightly unctuous.*"—ATHENÆUM.

"*The life of the Rev. Père Besson, who gave up an artist's career, to which he was devotedly attached, and a mother whose affection for him is not inaptly likened to that of Monica for St. Augustine, must be read in its entirety to be rightly appreciated. And the whole tenour of the book is too devotional, too full of expressions of the most touching dependence on God, to make criticism possible, even if it was called for, which it is not.*"—JOHN BULL.

"*The story of Père Besson's life is one of much interest, and told with simplicity, candour, and good feeling.*"—SPECTATOR.

"*A beautiful book, describing the most saintly and very individual life of one of the companions of Lacordaire.*"—MONTHLY PACKET.

"*We strongly recommend it to our readers. It is a charming biography, that will delight and edify both old and young.*"—WESTMINSTER GAZETTE.

The Life of Madame Louise de France,

Daughter of Louis XV., also known as the Mother Térèse de S. Augustin. By the Author of "A Dominican Artist," &c. New Edition. Crown 8vo. 6s.

"*Such a record of deep, earnest, self-sacrificing piety, beneath the surface of Parisian life, during what we all regard as the worst age of French godlessness, ought to teach us all a lesson of hope and faith, let appearances be what they may. Here, from out of the court and family of Louis XV. there issues this Madame Louise, whose life is set before us as a specimen of as calm and unworldly devotion—of a devotion, too, full of shrewd sense and practical administrative talent—as any we have ever met with.*"—LITERARY CHURCHMAN.

aterloo Place, London

The Revival of Priestly Life in the
Seventeenth Century in France : a Sketch. By the Author of "A Dominican Artist," "Life of S. Francis de Sales," &c. Crown 8vo. 9s.

"*A book the authorship of which will command the respect of all who can honour sterling worth. No Christian, to whatever denomination he may belong, can read without quick sympathy and emotion these touching sketches of the early Oratorians and the Lazarists, whose devotion we can all admire.*"—STANDARD.

Life of S. Francis de Sales. By the
Author of "A Dominican Artist," &c. Crown 8vo. 6s.

"*It is written with the delicacy, freshness, and absence of all affectation which characterized the former works by the same hand, and which render these books so very much more pleasant reading than are religious biographies in general. The character of S. Francis de Sales, Bishop of Geneva, is a charming one; a more simple, pure, and pious life it would be difficult to conceive. His unaffected humility, his freedom from dogmatism in an age when dogma was placed above religion, his freedom from bigotry in an age of persecution, were alike admirable.*"—STANDARD.

"*The author of 'A Dominican Artist,' in writing this new life of the wise and loving Bishop and Prince of Geneva, has aimed less at historical or ecclesiastical investigation than at a vivid and natural representation of the inner mind and life of the subject of his biography, as it can be traced in his own writings and in those of his most intimate and affectionate friends. The book is written with the grave and quiet grace which characterizes the productions of its author, and cannot fail to please those readers who can sympathize with all forms of goodness and devotion to noble purpose.*"—WESTMINSTER REVIEW.

"*A book which contains the record of a life as sweet, pure, and noble, as any man by divine help, granted to devout sincerity of soul, has been permitted to live upon earth. The example of this gentle but resolute and energetic spirit, wholly dedicated to the highest conceivable good, offering itself, with all the temporal uses of mental existence, to the service of infinite and eternal beneficence, is extremely touching. It is a book worthy of acceptance.*"—DAILY NEWS.

"*It is not a translation or adaptation, but an original work, and a very charming portrait of one of the most winning characters in the long gallery of Saints. And it is a matter of entire thankfulness to us to find a distinctively Anglican writer setting forward the good Bishop's work among Protestants, as a true missionary task to reclaim souls from deadly error, and bring them back to the truth.*"—UNION REVIEW.

The Last Days of Père Gratry. By PÈRE
ADOLPHE PERRAUD, of the Oratory, and Professor of La Sorbonne. Translated by Special permission. By the Author of "Life of S. Francis de Sales," &c. Crown 8vo. 3s. 6d.

Henri Perreyve. By A. Gratry, Prêtre

de l'Oratoire, Professeur de Morale Evangélique à la Sorbonne, et Membre de l'Académie Française. Translated, by special permission, by the Author of "A Dominican Artist," "Life of S. Francis de Sales," &c. &c. With Portrait. New and Cheaper Edition. Crown 8vo. 6s.

"*A most touching and powerful piece of biography, interspersed with profound reflections on personal religion, and on the prospects of Christianity. . . . For priests this book is a treasure. The moral of it is the absolute necessity of 'recollectedness' to the higher, and especially the true priestly life.*"—CHURCH REVIEW.

"*The works of the translator of Henri Perreyve form, for the most part, a series of saintly biographies which have obtained a larger share of popularity than is generally accorded to books of this description. . . . The description of his last days will probably be read with greater interest than any other part of the book; presenting as it does an example of fortitude under suffering, and resignation, when cut off so soon after entering upon a much-coveted and useful career, of rare occurrence in this age of self-assertion. This is, in fact, the essential teaching of the entire volume. . . . The translator of the Abbé Gratry's work has done well in giving English readers an opportunity of profiting by its lessons.*"—MORNING POST.

"*Those who take a pleasure in reading a beautiful account of a beautiful character would do well to procure the Life of 'Henri Perreyve.' . . . We would especially recommend the book for the perusal of English priests, who may learn many a holy lesson from the devoted spirit in which the subject of the memoir gave himself up to the duties of his sacred office, and to the cultivation of the graces with which he was endowed.*"—CHURCH TIMES.

"*It is easy to see that Henri Perreyve, Professor of Moral Theology at the Sorbonne, was a Roman Catholic priest of no ordinary type. With comparatively little of what Protestants call superstition, with great courage and sincerity, with a nature singularly guileless and noble, his priestly vocation, although pursued, according to his biographer, with unbridled zeal, did not stifle his human sympathies and aspirations. He could not believe that his faith compelled him 'to renounce sense and reason,' or that a priest was not free to speak, act, and think like other men. Indeed, the Abbé Gratry makes a kind of apology for his friend's free-speaking in this respect, and endeavours to explain it. Perreyve was the beloved disciple of Lacordaire, who left him all his manuscripts, notes, and papers, and he himself attained the position of a great pulpit orator.*"—PALL MALL GAZETTE.

Walter Kerr Hamilton, Bishop of Salisbury.

A Sketch by HENRY PARRY LIDDON, D.D., Canon of St. Paul's, and Ireland Professor of Exegesis in the University of Oxford. Second Edition. 8vo. 2s. 6d.; or with the Funeral Sermon, "Life in Death," 3s. 6d.

History and Biography

Life of S. Vincent de Paul. With Introduction by the Rev. R. F. WILSON, M.A., Prebendary of Salisbury and Vicar of Rownhams, and Chaplain to the Bishop of Salisbury. Crown 8vo. 9s.

"A most readable volume, illustrating plans and arrangements, which from the circumstances of the day are invested with peculiar interest."—ENGLISH CHURCHMAN.

"All will be pleased at reading the present admirably written narrative, in which we do not know whether to admire more the candour and earnestness of the writer or his plain, sensible, and agreeable style."—WEEKLY REGISTER.

"We trust that this deeply interesting and beautifully written biography will be extensively circulated in England."—CHURCH HERALD.

"We heartily recommend the introduction to the study of all concerned with ordinations."—GUARDIAN.

"We are glad that S. Vincent de Paul, one of the most remarkable men produced by the Gallican Church, has at last found a competent English biographer. The volume before us has evidently been written with conscientious care and scrupulous industry. It is based on the best authorities, which have been compared with praiseworthy diligence; its style is clear, elegant, and unambitious; and it shows a fine appreciation of the life and character of the man whom it commemorates."—SCOTTISH GUARDIAN.

"Mr. Wilson has done his work admirably and evidently con amore, and he completely proves the thesis with which he starts, viz., that in the life of the Saint there is a homeliness and simplicity, and a general absence of the miraculous or the more ascetic type of saintliness."—JOHN BULL.

John Wesley's Place in Church History
determined, with the aid of Facts and Documents unknown to, or unnoticed by, his Biographers. With a New and Authentic Portrait. By R. DENNY URLIN, of the Middle Temple, Barrister-at-Law, &c. Small 8vo. 5s. 6d.

A History of the Holy Eastern Church.
The Patriarchate of Antioch. By the Rev. JOHN MASON NEALE, D.D., late Warden of Sackville College, East Grinsted. A Posthumous Fragment. Together with Memoirs of the Patriarchs of Antioch, by Constantius, Patriarch of Constantinople; translated from the Greek, and three Appendices. Edited, with an Introduction, by the Rev. GEORGE WILLIAMS, B.D., Vicar of Ringwood, late Fellow of King's College, Cambridge. 8vo. 10s. 6d.

and at Oxford and Cambridge

History of the Church under the Roman Empire, A.D. 30-476.

By the Rev. A. D. CRAKE, B.A., Chaplain of All Saints' School, Bloxham. Crown 8vo. 7s. 6d.

"*A compendious history of the Christian Church under the Roman Empire will be hailed with pleasure by all readers of ecclesiastical lore. . . . The author is quite free from the spirit of controversialism; wherever he refers to a prevalent practice of ancient times he gives his authority. In his statement of facts or opinions he is always accurate and concise, and his manual is doubtless destined to a lengthened period of popularity.*"—MORNING POST.

"*It is very well done. It gives a very comprehensive view of the progress of events, ecclesiastical and political, at the great centres of civilisation during the first five centuries of Christianity.*"—DAILY NEWS.

"*In his well-planned and carefully written volume of 500 pages Mr. Crake has supplied a well-known and long-felt want. Relying on all the highest and best authorities for his main facts and conclusions, and wisely making use of all modern research, Mr. Crake has spared neither time nor labour to make his work accurate, trustworthy, and intelligent.*"—STANDARD.

"*Really interesting, well suited to the needs of those for whom it was prepared, and its Church tone is unexceptionable.*"—CHURCH TIMES.

"*As a volume for students and the higher forms of our public schools it is admirably adapted.*"—CHURCH HERALD.

"*We cordially recommend it for schools for the young.*"—ENGLISH CHURCHMAN.

"*Mr. Crake gives us in a clear and concise form a narrative of the Church history during the period with which it is most important that the young should first be made acquainted. The different events appear to be described with a judicious regard to their relative importance, and the manual may be safely recommended.*"—JOHN BULL.

"*The facts are well marshalled, the literary style of the book is simple and good; while the principles enunciated throughout render it a volume which may be safely put into the hands of students. For the higher forms of grammar-schools it is exactly the book required. Never ponderous, and frequently very attractive and interesting, it is at once readable and edifying, and fills efficiently a vacant place in elementary historical literature. Furthermore its type is clear and bold, and it is well broken up into paragraphs.*"—UNION REVIEW.

"*It retells an oft-told tale in a singularly fresh and perspicuous style, rendering the book neither above the comprehension of an intelligent boy or girl of fourteen or upwards, nor beneath the attention of an educated man. We can imagine no better book as an addition to a parochial library, as a prize, or as a reading book in the upper forms of middle-class schools.*"—SCOTTISH GUARDIAN.

Church Memorials and Characteristics;

being a Church History of the six First Centuries. By the late WILLIAM ROBERTS, Esq., M.A., F.R.S. Edited by his Son, ARTHUR ROBERTS, M.A., Rector of Woodrising, Norfolk. 8vo. 7s. 6d.

History and Biography

A Key to the Knowledge of Church
History (Ancient). Edited by the Rev. JOHN HENRY BLUNT M.A., F.S.A., Editor of "The Annotated Book of Common Prayer," &c. &c. Small 8vo. 2s. 6d.

Forming a Volume of "Keys to Christian Knowledge."

"*It offers a short and condensed account of the origin, growth, and condition of the Church in all parts of the world, from* A.D. 1 *down to the end of the fifteenth century. Mr. Blunt's first object has been conciseness, and this has been admirably carried out, and to students of Church history this feature will readily recommend itself. As an elementary work 'A Key' will be specially valuable, inasmuch as it points out certain definite lines of thought, by which those who enjoy the opportunity may be guided in reading the statements of more elaborate histories. At the same time it is but fair to Mr. Blunt to remark that, for general readers, the little volume contains everything that could be consistently expected in a volume of its character. There are many notes, theological, scriptural, and historical, and the 'get up' of the book is specially commendable. As a text-book for the higher forms of schools the work will be acceptable to numerous teachers.*"—PUBLIC OPINION.

"*It contains some concise notes on Church History, compressed into a small compass, and we think it is likely to be useful as a book of reference.*"—JOHN BULL.

"*A very terse and reliable collection of the main facts and incidents connected with Church History.*"—ROCK.

A Key to the Knowledge of Church
History (Modern). Edited by the Rev. JOHN HENRY BLUNT, M.A., F.S.A., Editor of "The Annotated Book of Common Prayer," &c. &c. Small 8vo. 2s. 6d.

Forming a Volume of "Keys to Christian Knowledge."

The Reformation of the Church of
England; its History, Principles, and Results. A.D. 1514-1547. By the Rev. JOHN HENRY BLUNT, M.A., F.S.A., Editor of "The Annotated Book of Common Prayer," &c. &c. Third Edition. 8vo. 16s.

Perranzabuloe, the Lost Church Found;
or, The Church of England not a New Church, but Ancient, Apostolical, and Independent, and a Protesting Church Nine Hundred Years before the Reformation. By the Rev. C. T. COLLINS TRELAWNY, M.A., late Rector of Timsbury, Somerset. New Edition. Crown 8vo. 3s. 6d.

and at Oxford and Cambridge

History of the English Institutions.
By PHILIP V. SMITH, M.A., Barrister-at-Law, Fellow of King's College, Cambridge. Crown 8vo. 3s. 6d.

Forming a Volume of "Historical Handbooks," edited by OSCAR BROWNING, M.A., Fellow of King's College, Cambridge.
[See RIVINGTON'S SCHOOL CATALOGUE.]

History of French Literature, adapted
from the French of M. Demogeot. By C. BRIDGE. Crown 8vo. 3s. 6d.

Forming a Volume of "Historical Handbooks," edited by OSCAR BROWNING, M.A., Fellow of King's College, Cambridge.
[See RIVINGTON'S SCHOOL CATALOGUE.]

The Roman Empire. From the Death
of Theodosius the Great to the Coronation of Charles the Great, A.D. 395 to A.D. 800. By A. M. CURTEIS, M.A., Assistant-Master at Sherborne School, late Fellow of Trinity College, Oxford. With Maps. Crown 8vo. 3s. 6d.

Forming a Volume of "Historical Handbooks," edited by OSCAR BROWNING, M.A., Fellow of King's College, Cambridge.
[See RIVINGTON'S SCHOOL CATALOGUE.]

History of Modern English Law. By
Sir ROLAND KNYVET WILSON, Bart., M.A., Barrister-at-Law, late Fellow of King's College, Cambridge. Crown 8vo. 3s. 6d.

Forming a Volume of "Historical Handbooks," edited by OSCAR BROWNING, M.A., Fellow of King's College, Cambridge.
[See RIVINGTON'S SCHOOL CATALOGUE.]

The Reign of Lewis XI. By P. F. Willert,
M.A., Fellow of Exeter College, Oxford. With Map. Crown 8vo. 3s. 6d.

Forming a Volume of "Historical Handbooks," edited by OSCAR BROWNING, M.A., Fellow of King's College, Cambridge.
[See RIVINGTON'S SCHOOL CATALOGUE.]

Waterloo Place, London

English History in the Fourteenth

Century. By CHARLES H. PEARSON, late Fellow of Oriel College, Oxford. Crown 8vo. 3s. 6d.

Forming a Volume of "Historical Handbooks," edited by OSCAR BROWNING, M.A., Fellow of King's College, Cambridge.

[See RIVINGTON'S SCHOOL CATALOGUE.]

Life of Robert Gray, Bishop of Cape

Town and Metropolitan of the Province of South Africa. Edited by his Son, the Rev. CHARLES GRAY, M.A., Vicar of Helmsley, York. With Portrait and Map. 2 Vols. 8vo. 32s.

"We have noticed this work at great length; but not, we venture to think, at a length that exceeds its merits and its interest. It is, in fact, more than a biography; it is a valuable addition to the history of the nineteenth century. Mr. Keble more than once described Bishop Gray's struggles as 'like a bit out of the fourth century.'"—GUARDIAN.

"The two volumes contain nearly twelve hundred pages; but the life which is here written is that of no ordinary man, and we do not know that we could wish a page omitted. The compiler has judiciously kept himself in the background. His own opinions are rarely given; his work has been limited to arranging the events of a stirring and devoted life, and throughout, by a felicitous selection of letters, we have the Bishop himself before us. His actions are related almost without comment, while the reasons for his actions are given in his own words."—SATURDAY REVIEW.

"There is a fascination in these volumes which few Churchmen will be able to resist."—JOHN BULL.

"We welcome it as a worthy tribute to the memory of one who possessed the true apostolic spirit, was a faithful son of the Church, and a distinguished ornament of the Episcopate."—STANDARD.

"Not only interesting as the record of a good man's life, but extremely valuable as materials for Church history."—CHURCH TIMES.

Life, Journals, and Letters of Henry

ALFORD, D.D., late Dean of Canterbury. Edited by his WIDOW. With Portrait and Illustrations. New Edition. Crown 8vo. 9s.

"On the whole, Mrs. Alford has acquitted herself admirably. . . . Those who desire thoroughly to appreciate a valuable life and a beautiful character we refer to the volume itself."—TIMES.

"It was a beautiful life he lived; and touchingly beautiful in its unadorned simplicity is the record given to us in this volume by his life-long companion, who from his early boyhood had shared his every thought."—GUARDIAN.

"We have here the simple and loving record of a happy, industrious, and holy life. . . . To have known and valued Henry Alford will long be a source of heartfelt satisfaction to many others, besides those immediate friends whose names are linked with his in this beautiful and touching Life by his widow."—SATURDAY REVIEW.

and at 𝔒xford an 𝔇ambridge

Historical Narratives. From the Russian.
By H. C. ROMANOFF, Author of "Sketches of the Rites and Customs of the Greco-Russian Church," &c. Crown 8vo. 6s.

Sketches of the Rites and Customs of
the Greco-Russian Church. By H. C. ROMANOFF. With an Introductory Notice by the Author of "The Heir of Redclyffe." Second Edition. Crown 8vo. 7s. 6d.

"*The volume before us is anything but a formal liturgical treatise. It might be more valuable to a few scholars if it were, but it would certainly fail to obtain perusal at the hands of the great majority of those whom the writer, not unreasonably, hopes to attract by the narrative style she has adopted. What she has set before us is a series of brief outlines, which, by their simple effort to clothe the information given us in a living garb, reminds us of a once-popular child's book which we remember a generation ago, called 'Sketches of Human Manners.'*"—CHURCH TIMES.

"*The twofold object of this work is* 'to present the English with correct descriptions of the ceremonies of the Greco-Russian Church, and at the same time with pictures of domestic life in Russian homes, especially those of the clergy and the middle class of nobles;' and, beyond question, the author's labour has been so far successful that, whilst her Church scenes may be commended as a series of most dramatic and picturesque tableaux, her social sketches enable us to look at certain points beneath the surface of Russian life, and materially enlarge our knowledge of a country concerning which we have still a very great deal to learn.*"—ATHENÆUM.

Fables respecting the Popes of the
Middle Ages. A Contribution to Ecclesiastical History. By JOHN J. IGN. VON DÖLLINGER, D.D., D.C.L. Translated by the Rev. ALFRED PLUMMER, M.A., Master of University College, Durham, late Fellow of Trinity College, Oxford. 8vo. 14s.

Curious Myths of the Middle Ages.
By S. BARING-GOULD, M.A., Author of "Origin and Development of Religious Belief," &c. With Illustrations. New Edition. Crown 8vo. 6s.

Reflections on the Revolution in
France, in 1790. By the Right Hon. EDMUND BURKE, M.P. New Edition, with a short Biographical Notice. Crown 8vo. 3s. 6d.

Waterloo Place, London

History and Biography

An English History for the Use of
Public Schools. By the Rev. J. FRANCK BRIGHT, M.A., Fellow of University College, and Historical Lecturer in Balliol, New, and University Colleges, Oxford; late Master of the Modern School in Marlborough College. With Numerous Maps and Plans. Crown 8vo.

> PERIOD I.—FEUDAL MONARCHY. The Departure of the Romans, to Richard III. A.D. 449-1485. 4s. 6d.
> PERIOD II.—PERSONAL MONARCHY: Henry VII. to James II. A.D. 1485-1688. 5s.
> PERIOD III.—CONSTITUTIONAL MONARCHY. William and Mary, to the present time. A.D. 1688-1837.

Historical Biographies. Edited by the
Rev. M. CREIGHTON, M.A., late Fellow of Merton College, Oxford. With Maps. Small 8vo. 2s. 6d. each.

> SIMON DE MONTFORT.
> THE BLACK PRINCE.

A History of England for Children.
By GEORGE DAVYS, D.D., formerly Bishop of Peterborough. New Edition. 18mo. 1s. 6d.

With twelve Coloured Illustrations. Square Crown 8vo. 3s. 6d.

The Annual Register: a Review of Public
Events at Home and Abroad, for the Years 1863 to 1875. New Series. 8vo. 18s. each.

and at 𝔒𝔵𝔣𝔬𝔯𝔡 and ℭ𝔞𝔪𝔟𝔯𝔦𝔡𝔤𝔢

10. Miscellaneous.

The Knight of Intercession, and other
Poems. By the Rev. S. J. STONE, M.A., Pembroke College, Oxford. Third Edition, revised and enlarged. Crown 8vo. 6s.

Yesterday, To-Day, and for Ever: A
Poem in Twelve Books. By E. H. BICKERSTETH, M.A., Vicar of Christ Church, Hampstead. Tenth Edition. Small 8vo. 3s. 6d.

A Presentation Edition with red borders. Small 4to. 10s. 6d.

"*We should have noticed among its kind a very magnificent presentation edition of 'Yesterday, To-day, and For Ever,' by the Rev. E. H. Bickersteth. This blank verse poem, in twelve books, has made its way into the religious world of England and America without much help from the critics. It is now made splendid for its admirers by morocco binding, broad margins, red lines, and beautiful photographs.*"—TIMES.

"*The most simple, the richest, and the most perfect sacred poem which recent days have produced.*"—MORNING ADVERTISER.

"*A poem worth reading, worthy of attentive study; full of noble thoughts, beautiful diction, and high imagination.*"—STANDARD.

"*In these light miscellany days there is a spiritual refreshment in the spectacle of a man girding up the loins of his mind to the task of producing a genuine epic. And it is true poetry. There is a definiteness, a crispness about it, which in these moist, viewy, hazy days is no less invigorating than novel.*"—EDINBURGH DAILY REVIEW.

"*Mr. Bickersteth writes like a man who cultivates at once reverence and earnestness of thought.*"—GUARDIAN.

The Two Brothers, and other Poems. By
EDWARD HENRY BICKERSTETH, M.A., Vicar of Christ Church, Hampstead. Second Edition. Small 8vo. 6s.

Waterloo Place, London

A Year's Botany. Adapted to Home
Reading. By FRANCES ANNA KITCHENER. Illustrated by the Author. Crown 8vo. 5s.

CONTENTS.

General Description of Flowers—Flowers with Simple Pistils—Flowers with Compound Pistils—Flowers with Apocarpous Fruits—Flowers with Syncarpous Fruits—Stamens and Morphology of Branches—Fertilization—Seeds—Early Growth and Food of Plants—Wood, Stems, and Roots—Leaves—Classification—Umbellates, Composites, Spurges, and Pines—Some Monocotyledonous Families—Orchids—Appendix of Technical Terms—Index.

[See RIVINGTON'S SCHOOL CATALOGUE.]

An Easy Introduction to Chemistry.
For the Use of Schools. Edited by the Rev. ARTHUR RIGG, M.A., late Principal of the College, Chester; and WALTER T. GOOLDEN, B.A., late Science Scholar of Merton College, Oxford. New Edition, considerably altered and revised. With Illustrations. Crown 8vo. 2s. 6d.

[See RIVINGTON'S SCHOOL CATALOGUE.]

A Shadow of Dante. Being an Essay
towards studying Himself, his World, and his Pilgrimage. By MARIA FRANCESCA ROSSETTI. With Illustrations. Second Edition. Crown 8vo. 10s. 6d.

"*The 'Shadow of Dante' is a well-conceived and inviting volume, designed to recommend the 'Divina Commedia' to English readers, and to facilitate the study and comprehension of its contents.*"—ATHENÆUM.

"*And it is in itself a true work of art, a whole finely conceived, and carried out with sustained power.*"—GUARDIAN.

"*We find the volume furnished with useful diagrams of the Dantesque universe, of Hell, Purgatory, and the 'Rose of the Blessed,' and adorned with a beautiful group of the likenesses of the poet, and with symbolic figures (on the binding) in which the taste and execution of Mr. D. G. Rossetti will be recognised. The exposition appears to us remarkably well arranged and digested; the author's appreciation of Dante's religious sentiments and opinions is peculiarly hearty, and her style refreshingly independent and original.*"—PALL MALL GAZETTE.

"*The result has been a book which is not only delightful in itself to read, but is admirably adapted as an encouragement to those students who wish to obtain a preliminary survey of the land before they attempt to follow Dante through his long and arduous pilgrimage. Of all poets Dante stands most in need of such assistance as this book offers.*"—SATURDAY REVIEW.

Hymns and other Verses. By WILLIAM BRIGHT, D.D., Canon of Christ Church, and Regius Professor of Ecclesiastical History in the University of Oxford. Second Edition. Small 8vo. 5*s*.

Parish Musings; or, Devotional Poems. By JOHN B. D. MONSELL, LL.D., late Vicar of S. Nicholas, Guildford, and Rural Dean. New Edition. Small 8vo. 5*s*.
    Also a Cheap Edition. Cloth limp, 1*s*. 6*d*.; or in paper cover, 1*s*.

Miscellaneous Poems. By HENRY FRANCIS LYTE, M.A. New Edition. Small 8vo. 5*s*.

The Elegies of Propertius. Translated into English Verse, by CHARLES ROBERT MOORE, M.A. Small 8vo. 2*s*. 6*d*.

The Iliad of Homer. Translated by J. G. CORDERY, late of Balliol College, Oxford, and now of H.M. Bengal Civil Service. Two Vols. 8vo. 16*s*.

English Nursery Rhymes. Translated into French. By JOHN ROBERTS, M.A., Fellow of Magdalen College, Cambridge. Square 16mo. 2*s*. 6*d*.

Physical Facts and Scriptural Record; or, Eighteen Propositions for Geologists. By the Rev. W. B. GALLOWAY, M.A., Vicar of St. Mark's, Regent's Park, Author of "Egypt's Record of Time," &c. 8vo. 10*s*. 6*d*.

Immanuel: Thoughts for Christmas and other Seasons, with other Poems. By A. MIDDLEMORE MORGAN, M.A. Small 8vo. 6s.

Mazzaroth; or, the Constellations. By FRANCES ROLLESTON. Royal 8vo. 12s.

Rivington's Devotional Series.

IN ELEGANT BINDINGS, SUITABLE FOR PRESENTS.

"To many persons there is something repulsive in a devotional volume unbound, and Messrs. Rivington have now turned their attention to the binding of their Devotional Library in forms that, like the books themselves, are neat, handsome, good, and attractive."—*The Bookseller.*

The Christian Year.

16MO. ELEGANTLY PRINTED WITH RED BORDERS.

	£	s.	d.
CALF or MOROCCO *limp, blind tooled*	0	5	0
THE SAME, ILLUSTRATED WITH STEEL ENGRAVINGS	0	6	6
THE SAME, ILLUSTRATED WITH A CHOICE SELECTION OF PHOTOGRAPHS	0	9	0
MOROCCO *superior*	0	6	6
RUSSIA *limp, gilt cross*	0	8	6
RUSSIA *limp, gilt lines and gilt cross*, ILLUSTRATED WITH A CHOICE SELECTION OF PHOTOGRAPHS	0	12	6
TURKEY MOROCCO, *limp circuit*	0	7	6
RUSSIA, *limp circuit*	0	9	0

The Christian Year.

CHEAP EDITION, WITHOUT THE RED BORDERS.

	£	s.	d.
FRENCH ROAN, *red inlaid or gilt outline cross*	0	1	6
THE SAME, ILLUSTRATED WITH STEEL ENGRAVINGS	0	2	6
FRENCH MOROCCO, *gilt extra*	0	2	0

The Imitation of Christ is also kept in the above-mentioned styles at the same prices.

The other Volumes of "The Devotional Series," viz.:—

Taylor's Holy Living
Taylor's Holy Dying
Wilson's Lord's Supper
De Sales' Devout Life
Herbert's English Poems and Proverbs

Can be had in a variety of elegant bindings.

Index.

	PAGE
ADAMS (WILLIAM), *Sacred Allegories*	72
———— *Warnings of the Holy Week*	54
A KEMPIS, *Imitation of Christ*	17, 25, 88
ALFORD (Dean), *Life, Journal, and Letters*	81
———— *Greek Testament*	7
———— *New Testament for English Readers*	7
ANDREWES (Bishop), *Manual for the Sick*	24
Angels, The Holy	40
Annotated Book of Common Prayer	2
———— *Compendious Edition*	1
Annual Register	83
ARNOLD (T. K.), *Sermons in a Country Village*	63
Ascetic Library: edited by ORBY SHIPLEY :—	
Mysteries of Mount Calvary	29
Counsels on Holiness of Life	29
Preparation for Death	29
Examination of Conscience	29
Athanasian Creed, Recent Theories considered, by G. D. W. OMMANNEY	5
———— "*Damnatory Clauses of,*" by MALCOLM MACCOLL	5
———— *Athanasian Origin of,* by J. S. BREWER	5
AVANCINI, *Vita et Doctrina Jesu Christi*	22
BAKER'S (W.), *Manual of Devotion for Schoolboys*	31
Bampton Lectures for 1865, by J. B. MOZLEY	42
———————1866, by H. P. LIDDON	47
———————1867, by E. GARBETT	45
———————1872, by J. R. T. EATON	62
———————1874, by STANLEY LEATHES	61
BARING-GOULD (S.), *Origin and Development of Religious Belief*	43
———— *Post-Mediæval Preachers*	33
———— *Curious Myths of the Middle Ages*	82
BARRETT (W. A.), *Flowers and Festivals*	34
———— *Chorister's Guide*	34
BARROW (G. S.), *The Mystery of Christ*	15
BEAMONT (W. J.), and CAMPION (W. M.), *Prayer Book Interleaved*	3
BEAVEN (JAMES), *Help to Catechising*	68
BICKERSTETH (Dean), *Catechetical Exercises on the Apostles' Creed*	68
———— *Questions Illustrating the XXXIX Articles*	68
————(E. H.), *Yesterday, To-day, and for Ever*	84
———— *The Two Brothers*	84

and at Oxford and Cambridge

	PAGE
BIRKS (T. R.), *Commentary on Isaiah*	10
BISHOP (C. K. K.), *Notes on Church Organs*	34
BLUNT (J. H.), *Annotated Prayer Book*	2
——— *Compendious Edition*	1
——— *Dictionary of Theology*	38
——— *Sects, Heresies, &c.*	39
——— *Directorium Pastorale*	33
——— *Doctrine of the Church of England*	39
——— *Sacraments and Sacramental Ordinances*	4
——— *Household Theology*	65
——— *Key to Church Catechism*	65
——— *History (Ancient)*	79
——— *(Modern)*	79
——— *Holy Bible*	15
——— *Prayer Book*	4
——— *Reformation of the Church of England*	79
——— and PHILLIMORE (W. G. F.), *Book of Church Law*	32
BODY (GEORGE), *Life of Justification*	48
——— *Temptation*	48
Bonn Reunion Conference, 1874 (*Report of*), Preface by H. P. LIDDON	45
Bossuet and his Contemporaries	73
BREWER (J. S.), *Athanasian Origin of the Athanasian Creed*	5
BRIDGE (C.), *History of French Literature*	80
BRIGHT (J. FRANCK), *English History*	83
BRIGHT (WILLIAM), *Faith and Life*	30
——— *Hymns and other Verses*	86
——— and MEDD (P. G.), *Liber Precum Publicarum*	2
BROWNING (OSCAR), *Historical Handbooks*. See under "*Historical.*"	
BRUTON (E. G.), *Ecclesiastical Dilapidations Act*	35
BURKE (EDMUND), *Reflections on the French Revolution*	82
CAMPION (W. M.), and BEAMONT (W. J.), *Prayer Book Interleaved*	3
CARR (ARTHUR), *Notes on S. Luke's Gospel*	8
CHILCOT (WILLIAM), *Evil Thoughts*	27
Christian Painter of the Nineteenth Century	73
——— *Year*	17, 23, 88
Church Builder	36
——— *Law, Book of*, by J. H. BLUNT and W. G. F. PHILLIMORE	32
——— *Organs*, by C. K. K. BISHOP	34
——— by F. H. SUTTON	34
CHURTON (W. R.), *Defence of the English Ordinal*	41
Clergy Charities, List of	36
CLERKE (Archdeacon), *Daily Devotions*	21
Companion to the Old Testament	10
——— *New Testament*	10
——— *Lord's Supper*, by the Plain Man's Friend	31
COMPTON (BERDMORE), *The Catholic Sacrifice*	55
Consoling Thoughts in Sickness	24
CORDERY (J. G.), *Translation of Homer's Iliad*	86
COSIN (Bishop), *Religion of the Realm of England*	41
CRAKE (A. D.), *First Chronicle of Æscendune*	71
——— *Second* ———	71
——— *History of the Church under the Roman Empire*	78
CRUDEN (ALEXANDER), *Concordance to the Bible*	16
CURTEIS (A. M.), *History of the Roman Empire, A.D.* 395-800	80

Index

	PAGE
DALE (T. P.), *Commentary on Ecclesiastes*	9
Dante, A Shadow of, by M. F. ROSSETTI	85
DAVYS (Bishop), *History of England*	83
DENTON (W.), *Commentary on the Lord's Prayer*	5
Dictionary of Theology, edited by J. H. BLUNT	38
———————— *Sects, Heresies, &c.* edited by J. H. BLUNT	39
DÖLLINGER (J. J. I. von), *Prophecies and the Prophetic Spirit*	40
———————— *on Reunion*	40
———————— *Fables respecting the Popes*	82
Dominican Artist, (A)	74
DUNCOMBE (Dean), *Family Devotions*	21
EATON (J. R. T.), *The Permanence of Christianity*	62
Ecclesiastes, Commentary on, by T. P. DALE	9
———————— *for English Readers,* by W. H. B. PROBY	14
ELLISON (H. J.), *Way of Holiness in Married Life*	63
FIELD (WALTER), *Stones of the Temple*	35
FLETCHER (JOSEPHINE), *Prayers and Meditations for Holy Communion*	20
FOSBERY (T. V.), *Hymns and Poems for the Sick and Suffering*	23
———————— *Voices of Comfort*	23
From Morning to Evening	24
GALLOWAY (W. B.), *Physical Facts and Scriptural Record*	86
GARBETT (EDWARD), *Dogmatic Faith*	45
GARLAND (G. V.), *Genesis, with Notes*	14
GEDGE (J. W.), *Young Churchman's Companion to the Prayer Book*	67
GODSON (J.), *A Vicar's View of Church Patronage*	46
GOULBURN (Dean), *Acts of the Deacons*	14
———————— *The Child Samuel*	18
———————— *Commentary on the Communion Office*	4
———————— *Farewell Counsels of a Pastor*	54
———————— *Family Prayers*	21
———————— *Gospel of the Childhood*	18
———————— *Holy Catholic Church*	37
———————— *Introduction to the Study of the Scriptures*	18
———————— *Manual of Confirmation*	69
———————— *Occasional Sermons*	54
———————— *Pursuit of Holiness*	18
———————— *Short Devotional Forms*	18
———————— *The Idle Word*	69
———————— *Thoughts on Personal Religion*	18
Gray, Life of Bishop	81
Gratry (Père), Last Days of, by PÈRE PERRAUD	75
———————— *Life of Henri Perreyve*	76
GRIMSTON (Sir HARBOTTLE), *Strena Christiana*	30
Guide to Heaven, edited by T. T. CARTER	19
GURNEY (AUGUSTUS), *Home Life of Jesus of Nazareth*	62
HADDAN (A. W.), *Apostolical Succession*	41
HALL (W. J.), *Psalms and Hymns*	6
———————— *New Mitre Hymnal*	6
———————— *Sermons on Various Subjects*	63

and at Oxford and Cambridge

	PAGE
Hamilton (Walter Kerr), a Sketch, by H. P. LIDDON	76
Help and Comfort for the Sick Poor	24
HERBERT (GEORGE), *Poems and Proverbs*	26, 88
HEURTLEY (Canon), *Parochial Sermons. Fourth Series*	63
HEYGATE (W. E.), *Allegories and Tales*	70
———— *The Good Shepherd*	31
Hidden Life of the Soul	17, 28
Historical Biographies, edited by M. CREIGHTON :—	
Simon de Montfort	83
The Black Prince	83
Historical Handbooks, edited by OSCAR BROWNING :—	
History of the English Institutions, by P. V. SMITH	80
———— *French Literature,* by C. BRIDGE	80
———— *the Roman Empire,* by A. M. CURTEIS	80
———— *Modern English Law,* by Sir R. K. WILSON	80
———— *The Reign of Lewis XI.,* by P. F. WILLERT	80
———— *England in the XIVth Century,* by C. H. PEARSON	81
HODGSON (CHR.), *Instructions for the Clergy, &c.*	33
HOLMES (R. R.), *Illuminated Edition of the Prayer Book*	3
Homer's Iliad, translated by J. G. CORDERY	86
HOOK (Dean), *Book of Family Prayer*	21
Hour of Prayer, with Preface by W. E. SCUDAMORE	21
HUTCHINGS (W. H.), *Mystery of the Temptation*	60
Hymnal, New Mitre, by W. J. HALL	6
Hymns and Poems for the Sick and Suffering, edited by T. V. FOSBERY	23
JACKSON (Bishop), *The Christian Character*	64
JAMES (Canon), *Christian Watchfulness*	30
———— *Comment upon the Collects*	5
———— *Evangelical Life*	30
———— *Spiritual Life*	30
JANUS, *The Pope and the Council*	46
JELF (Canon), *On the XXXIX Articles*	45
JONES (HARRY), *Life in the World*	63
———— *Priest and Parish*	33
———— *The Perfect Man*	63
JOYCE (J. W.), *Power of the Keys*	41
KAY (WILLIAM), *On the Psalms*	9
KEBLE (JOHN), *The Christian Year*	17, 23, 88
KENNAWAY (C. E.), *Consolatio, or Comfort for the Afflicted*	24
Keys to Christian Knowledge :—	
Key to the Four Gospels, by J. P. NORRIS	11
———— *Acts,* by J. P. NORRIS	11
———— *Holy Bible,* by J. H. BLUNT	15
———— *Prayer Book,* by J. H. BLUNT	4
———— *Church Catechism,* by J. H. BLUNT	65
———— *History (Ancient),* edited by J. H. BLUNT	79
———— *(Modern),* edited by J. H. BLUNT	79
KITCHENER (F. A.), *A Year's Botany*	85
LEATHES (STANLEY), *The Religion of the Christ*	61
———— *Witness of the Old Testament to Christ*	61
———— *St. Paul to Christ*	61
———— *St. John to Christ*	61

Index

	PAGE
LEE (WILLIAM), *Inspiration of Holy Scripture*	15
Liber Precum Publicarum, by W. BRIGHT and P. G. MEDD	2
Library of Spiritual Works for English Catholics:—	
À KEMPIS, *Of the Imitation of Christ*	17
The Christian Year	17
SCUPOLI, *The Spiritual Combat*	17
S. FRANCIS DE SALES, *Devout Life*	17
————————— *Spiritual Letters*	17
The Hidden Life of the Soul	17
LIDDON (H. P.), *Divinity of our Lord*	47
——————— *Elements of Religion*	47
——————— *University Sermons*	47
——————— *Walter Kerr Hamilton, In Memoriam*	76
——————— *Bonn Reunion Conference Report*, 1874	45
——————— *Andrewes' Manual for the Sick*	24
Light of the Conscience	28
Litanies, Metrical and Prose, A Book of,	3
LOUISE DE FRANCE, *Life of*	74
LYTE (H. F.), *Miscellaneous Poems*	86
LYTTLETON (Lord), *Private Devotions for School-boys*	23
MACCOLL (M.), "*Damnatory Clauses*" *of the Athanasian Creed*	5
MANT (Bishop), *Ancient Hymns*	29
——————— *Happiness of the Blessed*	42
Manuals of Religious Instruction, edited by J. P. NORRIS	66
MEDD (P. G.), *Household Prayer*	21
——————— and BRIGHT (WILLIAM), *Liber Precum Publicarum*	2
——————— WALTON H. B.), *Common Prayer, and Ordinal of* 1549	2
Meditations on the Life of our Lord, edited by T. T. CARTER	19
MELVILL (Canon), *Sermons*	56
——————— *Selections from Latter Sermons*	58
——————— *Sermons on Less Prominent Facts*	57
——————— *Lothbury Lectures*	59
MERCIER (A.), *Our Mother Church*	44
MEREWEATHER (J. D.), *Semele; or, the Spirit of Beauty*	72
MITCHELL J.), *On Church Government*	40
MOBERLY (Bishop), *Plain Sermons*	55
——————— *Great Forty Days*	55
——————— *Sermons at Winchester College*	55
MONSELL (J. D. B.), *Parish Musings*	86
MOORE (C. R.), *The Elegies of Propertius*	86
—— (DANIEL), *Aids to Prayer*	21
——————— *Sermons on Special Occasions*	59
——————— *The Age and the Gospel*	59
MORGAN (A. M.), *Immanuel and other Poems*	87
MOZLEY (J. B.), *Lectures on the Miracles*	42
——————— *University and other Sermons*	60
NEALE (J. M.), *Herbert Tresham*	72
——————— *The Virgin's Lamp*	22
——————— *History of the Holy Eastern Church*	77
NEWMAN (J. H.), *Parochial and Plain Sermons*	50
——————— *Lectures on Justification*	52
——————— *Sermons on Subjects of the Day*	53
——————— *Fifteen University Sermons*	53

and at 𝔒𝔵𝔣𝔬𝔯𝔡 and ℭ𝔞𝔪𝔟𝔯𝔦𝔡𝔤𝔢

	PAGE
NORRIS (J. P.), *Manuals of Religious Instruction*	66
——————— *Key to the Four Gospels*	11
——————— *Acts of the Apostles*	11
——————— *Rudiments of Theology*	67
OMMANNEY (G. D. W.), *On the Athanasian Creed*	5
OXENHAM (F. N.), *The Soul in its Probation*	60
PARNELL (FRANK), *Ars Pastoria*	33
Path of Holiness, edited by T. T. CARTER	19
PEARSON (C. H.), *English History in the XIVth Century*	81
PEPYS (Lady), *Morning Notes of Praise*	31
——————— *Quiet Moments*	31
PERRAUD (Père), *Last Days of Père Gratry*	75
Perreyve (Henri), by PÈRE GRATRY	76
PHILLIMORE (Sir R.), *Ecclesiastical Judgments, 1867-1875*	40
——————— (W. G. F.), and BLUNT (J. H.), *Book of Church Law*	32
PHILPOTTS (M. C.), *The Hillford Confirmation*	72
PIGOU (FRANCIS), *Faith and Practice*	64
POLLOCK (J. S.), *Out of the Body*	43
Prayer Book, American	3
——————— *Annotated*, by J. H. BLUNT	2
——————— *Illuminated*, by R. R. HOLMES	3
——————— *Interleaved*, by W. M. CAMPION and W. J. BEAMONT	3
——————— *Latin*, by W. BRIGHT and P. G. MEDD	2
——————— *of Edward VI., and Ordinal of* 1549	2
Prayers and Meditations for Holy Communion, by JOSEPHINE FLETCHER	20
Prayers for the Sick and Dying	24
PROBY (W. H. B.), *Ecclesiastes for English Readers*	14
——————— *Ten Canticles*	14
Psalter, or Psalms of David, pointed	5
PUSEY (E. B.), *Commentary on the Minor Prophets*	9
——————— *Lectures on Daniel the Prophet; with Notes*	9
QUESNEL, *Devotional Commentary on St. Matthew's Gospel*	14
QUIRINUS, *Letters from Rome on the Council*	46
RANKEN (W. H.), *Simple Sermons*	64
Reformation of the Church of England, by J. H. BLUNT	79
Revival of Priestly Life in the Seventeenth Century in France	75
RIDLEY (W. H.), *Bible Readings for Family Prayer*	16
RIGG (A.) and GOOLDEN (W. T.), *Easy Introduction to Chemistry*	85
Rivington's Devotional Series :—	
A KEMPIS, *Of the Imitation of Christ*	25, 88
DE SALES, *Devout Life*	25, 88
HERBERT (GEORGE), *Poems and Proverbs*	26, 88
WILSON (Bishop), *On the Lord's Supper*	26, 88
TAYLOR (JEREMY), *Holy Living*	27, 88
——————— *Dying*	27, 88
CHILCOT (WILLIAM), *Evil Thoughts*	27
The Christian Year	23, 88
ROBERTS (JOHN), *English Nursery Rhymes translated into French*	86
——————— (WILLIAM), *Church Memorials and Characteristics*	78
ROMANOFF (H. C.), *Historical Narratives from the Russian*	82
——————— *S. John Chrysostom's Liturgy*	45
——————— *Rites and Customs of the Greco-Russian Church*	82

	PAGE
ROLLESTON (FRANCES), *Mazzaroth ; or, the Constellations*	87
ROSSETTI (M. F.), *A Shadow of Dante*	85
SALES, S. FRANCIS DE, *Life*	75
———————— *Spiritual Letters*	44
———————— *Spirit*	28
———————— *Devout Life*	17, 25, 88
SCUDAMORE (W. E.), *Notitia Eucharistica*	4
———————— *Words to take with us*	20
SCUPOLI (LAURENCE), *Spiritual Combat*	17
Self-Renunciation, with an Introduction by T. T. CARTER	22
SHAW (MORTON), *The Position of the Celebrant*	30
SHIPLEY (ORBY), *Glossary of Ecclesiastical Terms*	68
———————— *Six Short Sermons on Sin*	63
———————— *Ascetic Library*	29
SHUTTLEWORTH (Bishop), *Last Three Sermons preached at Oxford*	64
Sickness, Consoling Thoughts in, edited by HENRY BAILEY	24
——— *its Trials and Blessings*	24
Sick, Andrewes' Manual for the, edited by H. P. LIDDON	24
Sick Poor, Help and Comfort for	24
——— *and Dying, Prayers for*	24
——— *and Suffering, Hymns and Poems for*, edited by T. V. FOSBERY	23
SINCLAIR (Archdeacon), *Thirty-two Years of the English Church* 1842-73	40
SLADE (JAMES), *Twenty-one Prayers for the Sick*	24
SMITH (P. V.), *History of the English Institutions*	80
Soimême ; A Story of a Wilful Life	70
Spiritual Guidance, with an Introduction by T. T. CARTER	22
Star of Childhood, edited by T. T. CARTER	19
STRACEY (W. J.), *Short Sermons on the Psalms*	62
STEPHENS (A. J.) *Argument in the case of Sheppard v. Bennett*	45
STONE (S. J.), *Knight of Intercession*	84
SUTTON (F. H.), *Church Organs*	34
TAYLOR (JEREMY), *Holy Living*	27, 88
———————— *Dying*	27, 88
Thirty-Nine Articles, by Canon JELF	46
———————— *Questions illustrating*, by Dean BICKERSTETH	68
Treasury of Devotion, edited by T. T. CARTER	19
TRELAWNY (C. T. C), *Perranzabuloe, The Lost Church Found*	79
URLIN (R. DENNY), *John Wesley's Place in Church History*	77
VINCENT DE PAUL, *Life of S.*, edited by R. F. WILSON	77
Voices of Comfort, edited by T. V. FOSBERY	23
WALTON (H. B.), and MEDD (P. G.), *Common Prayer, and Ordinal of* 1549	2
Way of Life, edited by T. T. CARTER	19
WEBSTER (WILLIAM), *Syntax and Synonyms of the Greek Testament*	15
Wesley's Place in Church History, by R. DENNY URLIN	77
WILLERT (P. F.), *Reign of Lewis XI.*	80

and at Oxford and Cambridge

	PAGE
WILLIAMS (ISAAC), *Devotional Commentary on the Gospel Narrative:*—	
Study of the Holy Gospels	12
Harmony of the Four Evangelists	12
Our Lord's Nativity	12
——— *Ministry* (2nd Year)	12
——— (3rd Year)	12
The Holy Week	12
Our Lord's Passion	12
——— *Resurrection*	12
——————— *Apocalypse*	13
——————— *Beginning of the Book of Genesis*	14
——————— *Characters of the Old Testament*	13
——————— *Female Characters of Holy Scripture*	13
——————— *Plain Sermons on the Catechism*	68
——————— *Sermons on the Epistles and Gospels*	49
WILSON (Bishop), *Sacra Privata*	30
——— *On the Lord's Supper*	26, 88
——— (Sir R. K.), *Modern English Law*	80
——— (R. F.), *Life of S. Vincent de Paul*	77
WORDSWORTH (Bp. CHARLES), *Catechesis*	68
——————— (Bp. CHR.), *Commentary on the Holy Bible*	8
——————————————— *Greek Testament*	8
——————————————— *Twelve Visitation Addresses*	62
——————————————— *Church of England and the Maccabees*	62
——————————————— *On the Inspiration of the Bible*	15
——————————————— *Intermediate State of the Soul*	45
——————————————— *Union with Rome*	45

www.ingramcontent.com/pod-product-compliance
Lightning Source LLC
Chambersburg PA
CBHW031945230426
43672CB00010B/2057